THE NEW IMPROVED AMERICAN

301.243
Asln

THE NEW IMPROVED AMERICAN

by Bernard Asbell

McGraw-Hill Book Company
New York
Toronto
London

To Paul,
young technologist and humanist,
who sees his two quests as one.

contents

7

forethoughts

The hardest thing about writing this book has been replying to friends who ask: "Oh, so you're writing a new one. What's it about?"

There should be a way of disposing of a subject in a word: "politics" or "medicine" or "marriage."

But for this subject I never found a word, or even a phrase, that did not have to be encased in qualifications, defenses and denials.

"It's sort of about automation," I'd say. Then shuddering at the sound of my own syllables, I'd add, "But no, it's not about machines. It's about the education of human beings."

"Oh, about education."

"Well, yes, but not really. It's more about mass ignorance and poverty."

"Oh, yes, of course, ignorance and poverty. Very timely.

9

Appalachia and so on."

"Well, when you put it that way, no. It's about how
people have stayed ignorant and poor because that was
the best way society could make use of them. But today
society can no longer use them in their ignorant state
and they're culturally trapped in ghettoes. They're useless, hopeless, frustrated and rebellious. That's what the
race riots are all about.

"Oh, I see. It's about civil rights."

"No, far from it. It's about automation and the need
for a new kind of education."

"My, you're a brave man to write a whole book on such
an *unhappy* subject."

"Oh, no. If anything, the book is too happy and optimistic. It will be criticized for that more than anything
else. But the gloomy side of automation has been amply
presented and needs no help from me."

On that confused note, the dialogue disintegrates.

The subject of this book is the biggest, most explosive,
yet most elusive domestic problem of our time. It defies
old labels. Most people not directly concerned with the
problem don't clearly know it exists. Those who are more
involved often describe it by abandoning words in mid-
sentence and turning to vague gestures.

I was invited recently to help plan a community conference of leaders called by the mayor of New Rochelle,
New York, a prosperous suburb troubled by an oversized,
segregated sub-suburb of uneducated, jobless fathers, a
disproportionate number of husbandless mothers, perilous
bands of mischievous adolescents, all victims of inherited
aimlessness. The town was further troubled by having
suffered a national publicity pounding during a local
political battle over racial desegregation of its schools.

"But what we want this conference to accomplish,"

said a keen, vibrant woman, a homemaker as well as
community leader, who was leading the planning discussion, "is to make our influential people understand that
the problem is more than just segregated schools, even
more than what's taught in schools. It's bigger. It has to
do with the disappearance of old jobs and creation of
new jobs, the obsolescence of old kinds of people and the
creation of new kinds of people. We have to start understanding the connections between the job issue and the
race issue, automation and education, dependency and
ambition. They're all part of—." Suddenly, at a loss for
words, the woman described a confused circle with her
hands and finally said, "—part of this whole new thing
happening in America."

That is precisely what this book is about.

One reason the problem remains undescribed, not to
mention unsolved, is that "experts" keep trying to pin old
labels on it. Each claims proprietorship of the problem by
giving it the name of his own expertness. Economists say
it's simply economics: Just stimulate the economy with a
tax cut here and a shot of purchasing power there and
there'll be work for all. Educators see it as a classroom
problem: We need mere remedial reading classes for the
young and labor retraining classes for the old. Social
workers feel that the poor need more personal counseling and they call for new studies to determine what kind
of counseling the poor need. Meanwhile industrial managers keep claiming that the thing we call automation is
nothing more than a steady continuation of the old industrial revolution which, after all, is what made America
great.

But seldom do these committed experts look beyond
the familiar categories and go out into the cities and
towns, the factories and mines, the Negro ghettoes and

slum schools, the newly mechanized farms and city unemployment offices, and look into the human face of
automation.

For three years I did this. I wanted human, nonstatis-
tical answers to important current questions. What kind
of people are not finding work? What did they do in the
past? What are they capable of learning to do in the
future? Why have they remained ignorant while others
have learned skills, even become educated? In a land of
free instruction, of wealth and opportunity, why are children by the hundreds of thousands headed down the same
road their parents traveled toward ignorance and poverty? Why do Negro teenagers, born to the age of computers, nuclear energy and moonshots, throw Molotov
cocktails at the cops? What can teachers do to absorb
these young minds into the mainstream of American opportunity and ambition? And finally, if all young people
were to do their homework preparing for high-level jobs
in an automated world, wouldn't matters be even worse?
After all, how many scientists, teachers, writers, programers, laboratory technicians can the world use? What will
we do with all these trained hands and educated minds
when machines are doing so much of the work?

There is a past as well as a future to man's adventure
among the machines he invents. We do not have to theo-
rize and guess; we can observe. I went to see men, women
and their children, not machines.

One of the people I saw was a school superintendent,
approaching retirement in a suburban community of
Georgia, his life a heap of newly-erupted conflicts: court
demands for school integration in the face of local demands to resist it; a national revolution in teaching
methods pitted against the conservatism of teachers and

parents; a growing need to prepare pupils en masse for jobs that no one could yet describe.

Yet the man was ebullient.

"Every age has its special excitement," he said, "and today's is right here in this spot where I am. When I walk down the street, among businessmen and civic leaders, I sometimes get the feeling they all ought to envy me.

"Permit me a personal anecdote," he said with Southern courtliness. "When my Granddaddy was eighty-two, that was right after World War I, he hitched up the wagon one day and took me to a fair. I'll never forget it. There was a great roar above me and for the first time I saw one of those early double-wing airplanes doing acrobatics in the sky. What a thrilling spectacle. The crowd was spellbound, watching. Everybody except Granddaddy. His sight was failing. He squinted and squeezed his old eyes, trying to focus them in the bright light. I tried to describe for him what was happening, but that was no good. He wanted to see it. Soon I began to cry for him. That poor old man. He had so little time left. He wanted so much to see that modern marvel, but his old eyes just wouldn't let him, and there was nothing I could do to help.

"That moment left a deep feeling in me. It comes back in a strange way when I think about us old-time educators in this new age we're in. We can hear the motors in the sky and we know that a marvelous thing is happening, but can we see it? Will the youngsters we are responsible for have to make it out for themselves and just cry for us old men? Or will we be able to do our jobs by helping them understand the meaning of what they see?"

That, too, is what this book tries to be about.

THE NEW IMPROVED AMERICAN

1

"a man ain't nothin' but a man"

In a factory in Michigan that makes automobile wheels, nothing but wheels, wheels, wheels, I recently saw a man who sits in a high perch beside a noisy, endless conveyor. All day unfinished wheels glide toward him from somewhere down the line, one about every ten seconds. He lifts each wheel from the conveyor, lays it down on a press, pulls a lever. The press smashes down on the wheel, leaving a decorative groove. The man lifts the wheel, puts it back on the conveyor, takes the next one.

Every ten seconds, every minute, every hour, every day, for year after year. The man's hair is gray, his eyes are gray, his skin is gray. His life appears gray. He sits atop his perch, waiting, waiting. He has been turning over wheels and pulling the lever how long? Since the day Franklin D.

Roosevelt died? Since the day Pearl Harbor was bombed? Since the day of the great Wall Street crash? Now he is at last getting old. His holy grail is almost at hand: soon a retirement plan will at last reward him by paying him a small allowance for not feeding wheels to the press. A simple, undemanding man, he will be free to fish, garden, drink beer, play pinochle, perform any simple, undemanding task while he waits out the short interval until it is time to die.

But I have not yet described the worst of the scene. Parallel to his conveyor, only five feet across an aisle where I stood watching, another conveyor had recently been installed. The new one is almost fully automatic. While on one side of me the man laboriously fed wheels every ten seconds, on the other side a robot on the automatic line fed wheels snappily, surely, at least twice as fast. Watching man and machine side by side I had a peculiar wish, perhaps a cruel one. I found myself hoping that the man's mind, after years of his stupefying task, had become blunted. That would protect him from a realization of the rhythmic, crushing accusation of the robot: *How easy this is, how easy this is, I do it better, I do it better, you've wasted your life, you've wasted your life, you slave, you slave, you slave, you slave. . . .*

Some of the most terrible poverty known in affluent America is endured today by the unemployed coal miner. If only we could be back to the good old days—so few years ago—before a robot called the "continuous miner" burrowed its way into the mines, scattering men in every direction, heaping them upon the slagpiles of the jobless.

In one of the best years of the good old days, 1947, a crew of 142 coal miners were hacking and shoveling, feeling their way around in the wet darkness that enveloped all their working lives in the No. 5 mine at Centralia, Illinois. Suddenly there was brilliant daylight. A roar rocked the tunnels. Some miners were killed instantly by the blast. Others perished more slowly from burns, bleeding, or the nonviolence of suffocation. In all, 111 had died before the rescuers came.

A few days later a reporter sat in a saloon near the ill-fated mine, talking to a well-scrubbed, neatly dressed young miner. The young fellow was saying, "I got a wife and one kid. Where else could I make thirteen-o-five a day? The railroads pay eight, nine dollars. And that's all there is around here. Sometimes I'd like to leave for good. But where'd I go? I don't know anything else. I don't like mining; it's not really life. I don't know what in hell you would call it. Well, it is a life, in a way too. I just wish my life away. When I go below I just wish it was tomorrow. Wish my life away. And I guess the others are the same way, too."

Those were the good old days of coal mining, before the machines came in and spoiled everything.

George Orwell has written of the lowliest laborers in restaurants of large hotels—before they were replaced by automatic dishwashers. These wretches were known in Paris as *plongeurs:* "Theirs is a job which offers no prospects, is intensely exhausting, and at the same time has not a trace of skill or interest; the sort of job that would always be done by women if women were strong enough. All that is required of them is to be constantly on the run, and to put up with long hours and a stuffy atmosphere. They have no way of escaping from this life, for they cannot save a penny from their wages, and working from sixty to a hundred hours a week leaves them no time to train for anything else. The best they can hope for is to find a slightly softer job as night-watchman or lavatory attendant.

"And yet the *plongeurs,* low as they are, also have a kind of pride. It is the pride of the drudge—the man who is equal to no matter what quantity of work. At that level, the mere power to go on working like an ox is about the only virtue attainable."

It is our national attitude to distrust the social consequences of any machine, no matter how marvelous, and to defend man's inalienable right to toil on like a beast of burden. To be grateful that a machine has relieved a man of his drudgery seems an act of betrayal.

When the mail brings a new checkbook with a peculiarly printed account number that can be read by machine, we don't breathe a sigh of relief for the human check sorter. We ask "What will become of people?" We bewail the fate of the species when the phone company tells us that seven-digit numbers will enhance the automatic operation of its switchboards. Not for the sake of unemployed phone operators, for there are none, but for the esthetics of the thing. One would think that human worth and dignity are built on a foundation of old-style two-letter telephone numbers.

This is an odd attitude for the most machine-minded nation in the world. Perhaps intellectuals romanticize the esthetic virtues of drudgery to free themselves from the guilt of performing none, while enjoying the fruits of drudgery performed by others. The laborer romanticizes his drudgery because that is the only way he can preserve his self-esteem.

To romanticize labor that is miserable, we even lie to ourselves, anything to draw beauty from the wretched.

This is what we do handsomely in the most durable and exciting of American folk songs.

We often describe our neglected heroes as "unsung," but surely the most "sung" hero in American history—taking the adjective literally—is a legendary Negro laborer from West Virginia named John Henry. Nine-tenths of all American Negroes, it has been said, are familiar with the "Ballad of John Henry" in some form. Among white people, the song has been spread widely, particularly among railroad workers in the Southeast, coal miners in West Virginia and Kentucky.

Among the schooled, too, the ballad enjoys a curious, growing fascination. In supper clubs, urbane folk singers perform it for urbane diners. In the recital hall, Richard Dyer-Bennet clips it out in British accents. Aaron Copland has composed an orchestral suite based on it. Even a modern jazz band, the Sauter-Finegan Orchestra, recorded it as a rhythmic recitation.

And what does the song say that enthralls such varied listeners? The simple ballad dramatizes, with overtones of classic tragedy, a contest between a man and a machine. During the drilling of the Big Bend Tunnel for the Chesapeake and Ohio Railroad near Talcott, West Virginia, John Henry was, according to the legend, king of the steel drivers. He hammered rods into the stone of a mountain to make holes for inserting explosives. The railroad one day introduced an automatic device, a steam-driven hammer, whereupon:

> *John Henry told his captain,*
> *"A man ain't nothin' but a man,*
> *But before I let your steam drill beat me down,*
> *I'll die with my hammer in my hand, Lord, Lord,*
> *I'll die with my hammer in my hand."*

His identity and dignity at stake, John Henry pounded "until his hammer was striking fire," and drove an accumulated length of fourteen feet of steel while the steam drill only made nine. Then, asking for a cool drink of water, he lay down his hammer and he died.

John Henry's triumph gratifies us all. It reassures us that man, the maker of wondrous mechanical things, is more wondrous than the things he makes. Yet while John Henry defeated the machine, the machine destroyed John Henry. As in classic tragedy, we are not quite sure if the hero won or lost. But there is no question that John Henry, swinger of a nine-pound hammer, stands for all that is good, and that the man who invented the steam drill ("He thought he was might fine, John Henry he drove fourteen feet, and the steam drill only made nine.") represents what is antihuman, the doer of evil.

The real importance of the song is that it is untrue. There was nothing poetic or glamorous or romantic about the real life or death of John Henry. He died an ignominious death, not at the scene of his historic race, but two years later in a rock blast in Big Bend Tunnel. He was thrown into a burial box with another Negro and dropped into the same grave as a third victim of the blast, a mule.

What good old way of life of John Henry's did the newfangled steam drill threaten? About a thousand men, mostly Negroes seven or eight years out of slavery, illiterate and untrained for anything better, toiled in the drilling of Big Bend Tunnel from 1870 to 1872. Nobody knows how many died from tunnel sickness (heat and foul air), explosions, or falls of rock, for there seemed to be a studied effort on the part of both the railroad and the local press to play down the casualties. But during the drilling of Big Bend, similar undertakings were yielding statistics of human destruction: 136 were killed in boring Hoosac Tunnel in Massachusetts, 1,000 in the drilling of Mont Cenis Tunnel through the French Alps. The drilling of Mont Cenis—where humans, like John Henry, performed the toil soon to be taken over by steam drills—was described in a magazine called *Every Saturday*, October 14, 1871:

"The smoke from the blast became so thick that the light from the lamps was visible no farther than a few steps. . . . Suddenly an infernal noise burst upon us from the end of the gallery. One would have said ten thousand hammers were falling simultaneously on their anvils. A sharp, whistling sound made itself heard above this clamor, piercing you to the very marrow."

Under conditions like these, in the good old days before steam hammers, John Henry labored at Big Bend for twelve, fourteen hours a day to do what the engineers said had to be done. America needed a new railroad to move west, and a mountain was standing in the way.

We are engaged, all of us, whether we know it or not, in history's most grand and pure act of humanity. We are making it unfeasible for masses of men to continue to live like animals. To those millions still entrapped in the animal pens of our old ways, we are showing the way—even compelling them down the way—to dignity, physical freedom and the joys of intellectual discovery.

Yet we speak of this act fearfully, ominously. Its name is pronounced with a gloomy ring of impending disaster. It is called *automation.*

The word is so forbidding, so inanimate, that at the sound of it I am tempted to clap the book shut myself. But stay. We will deal very little here with the obvious.

For one thing, nowhere will these pages describe a machine in detail, except as it may help dramatize the overturning of a human life.

For another, this book will not add to the cliché of extolling automation on the ground that it will bring abundance. On the other hand, neither will it join the chorus of (usually well-fed, well-clothed, well-heeled) spiritualists who wail, "Things, things, the world is already drowning in too many things."

For still another, there will be little concern here for the new billows of leisure which supposedly are soon to engulf us. On the other hand, there will be even less pondering of the kind of question that deep thinkers at cocktail parties are lately making fashionable: "Yes, but are ordinary working people *ready* for all that spare time?" (In fact, the book will present some evidence that work may soon occupy *more* time in the lives of more people, not less.)

The really important thing about the era of automation, which is already heavily upon us, is not machines or material abundance or long weekends. The subject of this book is the quality of the new, machine-shaped man. The subject is the new opportunity—in fact, the new *necessity* —for man to realize his own splendor. The argument here is that our new machines are finally forcing more of us into the grand quest of trying to discover ourselves as human beings.

The chapters are written mostly in the past tense, not in the conditional, subjective-case, future tense of the crystal ball that often is mistaken for sociology. This is not a speculation, but a report. For the deep, painful wounds often attributed to automation are already lying open all about us: unemployment, chronic poverty, malignant layers of ignorance, even the terrible awakening of open racial conflict. Anyone can see them who will dare to look.

But this book takes a risky stance—and will run its course in defense of itself—saying that these painful experiences are not at all the penalties of bringing on new machines. They are, in fact, the cruel evidences of our subhuman existence before the machines came. Each new public exposure of each old injustice is evidence that the situation of mankind is already getting better while it appears to be getting worse. Each dislocated life is a new demand that the dislocations must continue, as painlessly as we can manage, but continue until we altogether abolish our old ways of employing humans to do the work of uninvented, dumb machines.

A full generation—thirty-five years—ago, our country developed a mortal dread of unemployment as the worst thing that could befall the economic life of a man. And for good reason. When machines shut down, when factory gates clanked shut, men were entirely unprotected from being condemned to the mass uselessness, helplessness, and hopelessness, not to mention hunger, that on every hand befouled our streets.

The Great Depression left a permanent brand not only upon our national fears and aims, but upon our laws as well. Today a man is supposedly protected against having to descend below a certain level of misery. Social Security comes to the aid of the aged, unemployment compensation to the jobless; home relief saves families ineligible for the other aids, and Aid to Dependent Children shelters the babies of the widowed and unwed. There is some kind of protection against almost every possible calamity.

All except the one that is worst and most widespread. In times of economic panic, the immediate emergency may be unemployment. But in the long line of human history, we have been enchained, immobilized and retarded by the horrors of *employment*. We forget that it is not unemployment but employment that gives character and shape to what we are, the way we live, the kinds of nations we become. So grateful are we for the stultifying tasks that fill our working days that we overlook how empty they leave our lives. The failure of vast masses of men to fulfill the yet unimagined potentials of their minds and bodies is not the result of men's unemployment, but of the unnaturally confining demands of their *employment*.

Each system of production has a way of producing people appropriate to it, in approximately the numbers it needs them. The Indian way produces people who act like Indians, and a few who act like chiefs. The Soviet way produces people who act like collectivists and a few who act like commissars. The slave system produced people who acted like slaves, and, at an appropriate time in history, a few who acted like Harriet Tubman and Frederick Douglass. Similarly, the sharecropping system, the farm migrant system, the independent artisan system. And finally, our system of mass production on a beltline, mass addition and subtraction and clerking in cheerless offices, has produced, by the millions, people trained to dull their psyches, anesthetize their dreams, and passively submit their working lives to drudgery with no practical hope of escape from it.

The cause of unemployment today is not the lack of work to do. Not even a lack of economic means to put every man, woman, and child to work at useful tasks and still have a labor shortage. Far from it. The cause of today's unemployment is that we are emerging from a system of production—in the factory and on the farm—that required and produced millions of people of such inferior capability, such limited horizons, such faint ambitions, that they are too retarded to assume the more sophisticated tasks demanded of them today. The tasks will

get more sophisticated all the time. Which means our
new system—called automation—by its nature will require
us to produce more sophisticated people all the time.

Yet we deplore it. In condemning machines as the *cause*
of unemployment, we imply that progress is in the direction of going back to dumb, old-style men harnessed to
dumb, old-style machines.

As you read through these pages about some of the
consequences of robots and computers, you are asked to
lay aside a passion so deeply ingrained it is almost
instinctual. You are asked to suspend the fear of
unemployment as the worst of economic fates. Just for a
while. By doing so, one is freer to consider, perhaps for the
first time, the fearful consequences of what men have been
employed to do. This is an attempt to take a fresh look at
the familiar, as though it were a strange land.

Perhaps we can take new measure of the cruelties our
past has perpetrated in the name of work, of job security,
of prosperity. And perhaps we will begin to regard the
unhuman laborer, the machine, for the first time in an
unfamiliar light—as a great humanizer. For the first time
in history, machines require that masses of men be not
stupid but smart. They must be literate, instructed,
trained. The abolition of ignorance is no longer a matter of
mere social justice. It is a matter of economic survival.
When his survival is the issue, man acts.

We are already acting. President Lyndon B. Johnson
responded neither with light words nor with light inten-
tions when he declared, during his first days in office, a
massive and final "war on ignorance." But let us not make
the error of lumping President Johnson's war with other
kinds of wars, and missing the point of what a special kind
of war this is. This is not like a "war on unemployment,"
won by creating unnecessary work projects in the hope

that "things will get normal again." Certainly it is not like a war against enemy nations, in which our best men kill their best men, and nobody wins.

This is a war that everybody wins. In our busy-ness to alleviate the immediate pains of poverty and ignorance, let's not forget to rejoice at the meaning of it all. What we are saying is that today's economic problems are of so peculiar a nature that the way to solve them is to make men better.

To be even more optimistic, the literacy, instruction, and training forced upon the multimillions by robots and computers may be the first invitation for many to venture into that mysterious, uncharted, ethereal place that we vaguely but reverently call *education*. That is a good thing to happen. If a living person can be invited by a machine to enter the highest of civilized states, perhaps machines are indeed becoming, as those who dread them often wail, almost human.

2

the picking-up and putting-down machine

One morning in the opening days of the sixties, newspaper readers were jarred over their breakfast coffee when they read a solemn warning that in the next twenty years robots and computers might assume virtual command over American life in a "silent conquest." The dark fantasy, disguised in the ponderous prose of scholarliness, was written by Donald N. Michael, a "planning consultant," and published by the Ford Foundation's offshoot, the Fund for the Republic. A *New York Times* editorial called it a "gloomy report of an automated world in which people will be consigned to the junk heap."

The very next morning, *Times* readers were jarred again, this time by a lavish advertisement, seven columns wide, offering for sale an honest-to-goodness robot. The ad was not hidden, as one might expect, in the financial section, but boldly displayed amidst the general news, alongside ads for lingerie, love seats, and Florida vacations.

"TransfeRobot 200," the ad announced cheerily, "is a revolutionary general-purpose automation device designed to work on any assembly line. . . . Under the direction of its own electronic brain . . . it can perform one type of operation for a week, a month or a year, and then be reprogrammed. . . . TransfeRobot 200 will pick up, turn over, insert, transfer, shuttle, rotate, or position parts accurately, and will control secondary operations, such as drilling, stamping, heat sealing, welding, embossing, forging."

The thought of such robots appearing on assembly lines everywhere—working faster than people, better than people, and more cheaply than people—gladdened at least one reader. He was the inventor of the marvelous machine, the modern counterpart of John Henry's villain, "the man who invented the steam drill who thought he was mighty fine."

Since the "silent conquest" of machines over men is perpetrated in minds such as his, perhaps we should begin our journey through the real world of automation by getting to know him.

When he invented the TransfeRobot, John DeWitte Goodell of Silver Spring, Maryland, was fifty-two and employed as president of the Automation Division of U.S. Industries, Inc., a multimillion-dollar amalgam of automation equipment producers. He had previously invented a magnetic "decision maker" that is now a basic component of many computers, and a "memorizing" machine to teach people anything that can be learned by rote, from multiplication tables to French vocabulary. He has even invented an automation machine to teach workers how to operate other automation machines.

When I suggested to Goodell that these achievements would seem to qualify him as the villain of the piece, his characteristic poise went up in smoke.

"Why do the economists keep making the automation inventors look like the villains?" he demanded. "The basic problem presented by automation is how to distribute all the goods to all the people who need them. That's a problem for the economists. Why don't they solve that instead of pointing a finger at us?"

Goodell upsets the stereotyped image of the machine-worshiping robot inventor. Start a discussion with him about efficiency and he switches you to talking about education; start on machines and he twists the discussion around to people. While it is supposed that he wants to throw everybody and his brother out of work, Goodell pronounces the word "work" joyfully, as if it were another word for "love." When he talks about work he can't sit down. His tall, thin, slightly hunched frame begins to bob and he scurries about the room.

"Today the word 'work' describes something undesirable," he declares. "It will soon be redefined. Most people work just to make money. Then they spend it trying to buy happiness. But if we have challenging jobs that make us happy, we have a short cut. I've had people working for me who found work more desirable than almost everything else."

Not long ago, Goodell was commissioned to install a TransfeRobot to replace a person engaged in what he would call undesirable work. In a candy factory in Brooklyn, he studied a middle-aged, rotund woman scooping handfuls of chocolates from a tray and inserting them

into holes in a dial table. The circular table spun with a
rapid, stuttering motion so that three times every second a
new empty slot snapped before her to be filled with a
chocolate. With the intent hands and bowed head of Van
Cliburn playing a searing cadenza, the woman positioned
the candies at the speed demanded by the machine, every
now and then missing a hole, crossing her hands in a
terpsichorean design, breaking her rhythm to fill the hole
before it got away, yet not losing her pace in stuffing the
slots that unceasingly stuttered before her. Eight hours a
day she concentrated the wondrous mechanisms of her
body and brain on the speedy, repetitive feeding of
chocolates to the insatiable, spinning table.

"All the way back home on the train to Silver Spring,"
says Goodell, "I was so depressed I was sick. I couldn't get
that woman out of my mind."

Goodell responded to the woman's plight in the best
way he knew—by trying to eliminate her job. He not only
rigged a TransfeRobot to take over the woman's chocolate-
feeding task but arranged a line of them to perform the
repetitive tasks of thirty-nine other women who devote the
best hours of their days to picking up candies here and
putting them down there as speedily as machines can make
them move. Goodell was not sure whether these forty
women were to be moved to other tasks or fired, whether
they would find other jobs or be cast among the growing
heap of chronically unemployed. He manages to stay un-
troubled by the prospects of immediate consequences,
sustaining himself in the secure belief that in the long
run he is improving the human condition. If machines do
the dull, dreary things that people now do, people will
learn to do better things. He considers himself a bene-
factor of those forty women at the candy factory.

Repetitive labor, like that of the chocolate-feeding

woman, had inspired the invention of the TransfeRobot in the first place. An officer of U. S. Industries, Edwin F. Shelley, had been struck one day with the realization that thousands upon thousands of people spend all their working days in a maneuver that is highly useful, but hardly more demanding of their full talents than thumb-twiddling. They pick something up, and, a few inches away, put it down—feeding it into a machine, or inserting it into a hole or packing it in a box. If a set of "fingers" were custom-designed to handle each object, a machine could be produced that would be easily adapted to any such drudgery. Shelley built a mock-up robot, but realized it was too big and complicated. He turned the idea over to Goodell.

"John is the kind of fellow," says one of his engineering friends, "who can stare at a windmill, dismantle it, put the pieces back together in an unexpected way, and come up with a racing car."

That's just about what he did. Goodell was fretting over the robot problem one day when his eye was caught by his secretary's I B M electric typewriter. As she typed, its carriage would slide out like the reach of an arm, retract, then start reaching out again. Here were the makings of a precise, obedient reaching machine, carefully engineered and "debugged." All the arm needed was a "hand," equally precise and obedient, for picking up at one end of the reach, and putting down at the other. Goodell seized the typewriter from his bewildered secretary, took it apart and began building the first standardized, multipurpose robot of the automation era. It is housed in a starkly simple metal box, about the size of a typewriter. Its "reaching arm," in another plain box, slides to and fro, clicking efficiently, along the top.

Goodell equipped his TransfeRobot with an electronic

brain, so that TransfeRobots can be organized in committees, do separate tasks, and "talk" to one another. One robot can tell another, "I have just done my task, now do yours." The last one can tell the first, "The job's all done, so start over again."

Besides packing chocolates, TransfeRobots are in use assembling steering wheels, feeding tiny watch parts to a precision drill, even squirting droplets of oil into the bearings of clocks. They not only save time, but prevent injuries. A company in Massachusetts bought one the day after an employee, feeding small parts to a hazardous press, had his fingers cut off.

It may chagrin the I B M people to know that one of the first TransfeRobots, with its I B M typewriter parts, was sold to the Underwood people to assemble Underwood typewriter parts. If this seems like a surprising degree of inbreeding, the TransfeRobot can go even further. If TransfeRobots are ever mass produced, as Goodell believes they may be, TransfeRobots can be used to help make other TransfeRobots.

Another machine, hatched, in a different sense, by an automation machine is Goodell's invention called the Digi-Flex. It retrains workers displaced by a machine to operate the machine that displaced them. The Post Office Department had just begun testing a marvelous device—not designed by Goodell—to abolish the hand sorting of mail. Letters pass on a rapid conveyor before a clerk's eyes; the clerk is supposed to press a combination of pianolike keys to drop each letter in its proper sorting bin. But supervisors of training were having an awful time teaching the clerks to "play the chords" right. The Post Office called in Goodell. He applied a reflex principle in designing the DigiFlex. The machine flashes an address, and the proper combination of keys presses *up* against the clerk's fingers,

as though shouting, "Me! Me! Press me!" Goodell's simple
principle is that when something presses against a finger,
the finger wants to press back. When a trainee hits a wrong
key, the DigiFlex scolds him instantly by flashing a red
light. Post Office officials noticed an immediate upsurge in
alertness by trainees. Next, Goodell wants to adapt the
DigiFlex to teaching touch typewriting and musical sight
reading on the piano.

The DigiFlex, of course, does not solve all the education
problems of mail sorters. Many still must memorize thousands of addresses and know instantly which of hundreds
of sorting bins an address belongs in. So Goodell and an
assistant invented the MemoTutor to speed any kind of
simple rote learning: not only multiplication tables and
French vocabulary, but football plays, price lists, scientific
formulas, telephone extension numbers, shorthand symbols, an infinite number of things. In teaching, say,
French vocabulary, the machine shows the student a
French word and its English equivalent, then another,
and another. Then the machine begins to test the student.
If the student gets a word wrong, the machine scolds him
by flashing that abominable red light. But when the
student keeps getting a word right, the machine automatically drops the word from its curriculum and substitutes a new one. Thus the machine teaches, simultaneously tests, and automatically expands the course of
study, all at a speed set by the ability of the individual
student. Goodell is pained by the thought of a French
teacher being wasted teaching French vocabulary when
she could delegate that low function to a machine, and
free herself to teach the nuances of French grammar.

While many of his colleagues see little connection
between automation in teaching and automation in the
factory, Goodell regards them as twins. They both relieve

humans from dull, repetitive jobs, freeing them for more challenging ones. He also regards machines that teach as a short cut to raising the skills of people whose factory jobs are taken over by robots.

The immediate problem that concerns Goodell is not a dangerous surplus of workers, but a dangerous shortage of teachers.

"My five children," he protests, "attend classes that are too big because there aren't enough teachers. They need more help with their homework than I have time to give them. The shortage of good teachers is getting worse all the time. That's one of the problems that got me interested in machines that teach."

It may seem odd that Goodell should be so preoccupied with the problem of schooling, for he has had little of it himself. Yet a consuming force in his life has been a conflict over learning—an intense drive to learn and an equally intense resistance to the dull routines of learning.

Goodell's first rebellion against repetitive, mind-dulling drudgery came at the age of eight. He spent many of his evenings in a silent-film theater where he was given free admission in exchange for pumping the player piano. After a while he could hardly stand the monotony of pumping the piano but he was not prepared to give up the pleasures of seeing the movies. He studied how the piano worked and devised a way of automating it to heighten the drama on the screen. He punched holes in the standard music rolls to make them more appropriate to the action. As an example, for avalanche scenes he added perforations to produce rumbling, ominous low notes; for love scenes he superimposed romantic trills.

But still the music rolls had to be pumped. He decided to give up the boredom of his movie career in favor of becoming a juggler. That's when he learned how one must

invest unbelievably dreary practice, hour upon hour, day
upon day, week upon week, to learn an advanced muscular
skill. He decided there must be a way to cut through the
thick walls of drudgery for more direct access to artistry
and delight.

He investigated his hunch at the age of ten by designing
—on paper—a machine that would perpetually keep three
balls juggling in the air. He became convinced that the
machine would juggle better than he could learn to do, so
why learn? But he could not imagine an audience offering
thrilled applause at watching a machine juggle, so why
build the machine? This philosophical paradox was too
much for a ten-year-old mind. John renounced all interest
in juggling.

After running away to New York young Goodell
enrolled in a high school that permitted students to cut
classes without an excuse if they attained an average of 90.
With ease he hit 92.5—with such ease, in fact, that he
decided there are better ways to learn than going to
school. He has never earned a high-school diploma.

He landed the job he wanted most in the world—as a
theater organist—but soon became fascinated with the
prospect of automating himself out of that job. Talking
pictures were coming in, and with them musical sound
tracks. By spending spare hours in projection booths,
Goodell learned the principles of sound on film, and set to
work applying those principles to the invention of an
electronic organ. The idea of losing a job he loved to a
machine of his own invention seemed not a threat but a
kind of relief. If he could make an organ play itself as well
as he could play it—perhaps better—he could learn to do
something else, perhaps better than organ playing. He
built an electronic organ, brought the idea to the Radio
Corporation of America, and young Goodell (he was not

yet twenty) learned to his dismay that an almost identical invention had just been patented by a well-known electronics engineer.

That was all right. He was already developing a new interest. In a science journal he read of a then new invention called the electroencephalograph, a delicate device for recording brain waves. He built a rudimentary one that worked, hoping to analyze mathematically what brain waves mean. To this day scientists have not accomplished that task, but Goodell is still working at it. He believes that that puzzle, when solved, will reveal some unknown but startling short cut to learning—without drudgery.

Goodell's distaste for drudgery frequently took the form of not bothering to stuff his head with information—even important information—that he knew he could easily obtain if he needed it. At the outbreak of World War II, Goodell applied for a civilian job with the Army Signal Corps in Detroit. An interviewer asked him a stock question, "How would you align a superheterodyne radio circuit?" It was a question that any good radio repair man could answer, but it caught Goodell entirely flatfooted. He was prepared to razzle-dazzle the interviewer with advanced know-how, but hardly anything elementary. Goodell replied, "I'd get a good book on the subject and read it." The interviewer, taken aback, mused, "That's a very unusual answer." He hired Goodell on trial. Six months later, Goodell, with no high-school diploma, was appointed to coordinate the work of more than a hundred graduate engineers.

The experience helped Goodell solidify his impatience with much of present-day education. He believes that we teach students to waste themselves by teaching them to imitate machines. Just as the lady feeding candies to the dial table imitated a completely unintelligent robot, we make our students imitate mere computers. All a computer can do, Goodell argues, is to memorize more information than people can, and add thousands of times faster. Goodell considers this a minor talent that should be delegated to computers at every opportunity—leaving the minds of men clear to think of what they want done.

"I wouldn't dream of memorizing facts if I can put them into a computer and call on them when I need them," he protests. Yet, he believes, our whole educational system, a hangover from the precomputer era, rewards the learning of mere fact and discourages the pursuit of curiosity.

Perhaps Goodell's life-long impatience with drudgery foreshadows how most people will feel when robots and computers are widely engaged in the work that now so widely engages man. If that is so, then perhaps he also foreshadows the paths that many men's minds will take when they are freed from imitating machines. The more he explored a far-ranging interest in ideas, the more he felt himself bumping into islands of ignorance. He developed a consuming desire for fundamental theoretical learning. Mastering one science wasn't enough; he wanted to search for what he calls the "connective tissue" between all the sciences. Instead of specializing, he wanted to be a "general practitioner." If inventing was to be his trade, then he could *really* invent.

At the age of forty Goodell undertook a vast study of basic mathematics, logic, philosophy, physiology, psychology. While he designed products for the commercial electronics market by day, he spent two years of evenings burrowing, line by line, through *Principia Mathematica*, by Alfred North Whitehead and Bertrand Russell, a celestial three-volume work of intimidating equations and comparatively few English words. Because this was an important drudgery that could not be delegated to a machine, Goodell reasoned to himself, it was worthy of a good man's attention.

"The first time I saw him," says John Lockridge, a mechanical designer who assisted on some of his automation inventions, "we were about to start work on the DigiFlex and he was explaining his concept. He got all wound up in Pavlov's reflex experiments, the structure of the nervous system, the workings of the brain, stuff I never expected to hear an engineer talk about. I had to go out and buy books and cram like hell to try to keep up."

In studying the mathematical theories of games, Goodell came across an ancient Oriental game called "Go." Its rules are simpler to learn than those of checkers, but success in the game requires grand strategy and complex tactics.

Goodell would like to invent a computing machine that could play Go. "Each move," he says, "has such involved ramifications that any machine capable of sorting them out would do what amounts to creative thinking. The machine would be so smart you could feed it engineering data and it would invent other machines."

If a machine-inventing machine were ever invented, Goodell believes, it would lack only one thing—and here he invokes a word he rarely uses—a soul. A machine could not be taught to care.

"True," he says, "a machine can be made to do anything physical a man can do. But it takes a man to give things purpose and to be happy doing things. I can't imagine, for example, a machine that would enjoy going to the theater with me. Nor can I imagine a machine that would enjoy playing Go. As long as that's true, man doesn't have to fear machines."

To come back to the immediate realities of the automated world of John Goodell, what ever happened to those forty women at the candy factory? Were they, like the imagined victims of the "silent conquest," consigned to the junk heap?

As it turned out, the candy company changed its mind about investing in an assembly line of robots, so we don't know what would have been the fate of the women if they had.

That is poetically appropriate. It enables us to say we don't know what would have happened *if* ——. The truth is that when machines are indeed put into action, we usually don't know what happens as a result to the jobs of people. We only talk as though we do.

We keep talking about machines "replacing" people, *i.e.*, forcing the "replaced" people into unemployment, when the truth is they hardly ever do. The candy factory was a large one, employing hundreds upon hundreds, and was growing. The managers intended—or so they told me —to place those forty women in other jobs that needed filling, jobs not made up of the ceaseless repetition that robots are ready to perform.

Similarly, the man in the perch at the auto-wheel factory was not replaced by a robot. He was augmented by one. The old-fashioned machinery he operates still has valuable life in it. His employer cannot be so wasteful as to throw it out. But when business kept getting better and the plant had to grow, it was cheaper to put in an additional machine that was manless, instead of one that had to be equipped with another wage-earning man. When the old machine finally wears out, surely it will be replaced by a manless one. But by then, the man who runs it will have retired. No one will be fired. The old man merely will not be replaced.

So the man "displaced" by a robot is usually not the man whose work it does, but someone else who comes to the employment window looking for a job and is told, "Sorry, nothing today."

Even this does not happen as often as one might think. It's wrong to assume that for every job assigned to a machine there is a jobless worker out in the street. Far from it. Over the past hundred years machines have proliferated from John Henry's steam-driven hammer to John Goodell's electronic-brain TransfeRobot, yet jobs have multiplied.

When a Brooklyn candymaker invests in a robot, these things happen:

First, he must order the machine. This pumps money through the payroll of the robot maker, the robot maker's suppliers, the bank that finances the robot, the trucking companies that deliver it. So factories, offices, and transportation have been enlivened even before the robot is plugged in and the worker thrown out.

Next, the robot goes to work. It works more cheaply than a worker, so the employer may make a bigger profit. He may put his profit into a savings bank. The bank will lend the money to an expanding business which uses it to hire new help. Or the bank may lend it to a family building a home, and a building contractor hires help. But the employer seldom does that; bank interest rates don't attract him. The chances are he'll invest in expanding his own business or start a new one—in either case creating more jobs. But the employer may not do either. If the robot turns out chocolates so much more cheaply, the boss may cut the price of his chocolates in the hope of knocking out his competition. When the price comes down, more people buy—and more jobs are created to make them, pack them, sell them, advertise them, and total up the bills. The production of ball-point pens and television sets provides two examples of automation bringing down prices and boosting employment.

But the economic work of the robot still is not done.

After the profits of the robot trickle into the pockets of so many people, these people spend the money. They can't spend it all on reduced-price chocolates. So they buy hams and honey, books and boats, tickets to ballets and circuses, inviting guests in and having Sunday dinner out. These are items that can hardly be produced by robots. Some are not items at all; they are services, which now provide *more than half* of all the jobs in America. The strange procedure of machines creating jobs by "putting workers out of work" has inflated our labor market like a mammoth balloon to 70 million jobs, and the number keeps enlarging.

Machines create far more jobs than they destroy. That is a law of history, quoted tiresomely; everybody knows it, but almost nobody believes it when the issue stares us in the eyes.

But that law has one big *if:* machines provide jobs for men *if* there are men capable of filling them. For the jobs that machines create are usually not the same kind the machines destroyed.

We make the error too often of talking about the "labor market"—about 70 million jobholders and jobseekers—as though all workers were the same, like so many interchangeable pins in a pegboard. An officeholder says in alarm that we must create a million new jobs a year. What kind of jobs? Mopslingers or missile experts? Why not say we must train a million unemployed a year for unfilled jobs that already exist? An electrical union fights impending unemployment by bargaining for a 25-hour week. But electricians are not among the chronically unemployed. If more jobs are created for electricians, the unemployed coal miner will still be out of work.

Then who is the man who gets told at the employment window, "Sorry, nothing today"? If we can draw his profile, we know something about the man who is really displaced. We might go still further and get him back to work at a better job than he ever had.

The profile is not hard to draw. In a word—a blunt one —he is a primitive. His trouble is not brought about by automation. Automation is merely bringing his discomfort into the open, disturbing the comfort of the rest of us. We have been comfortable in the illusion that, until the new machines came, he was in good shape because there were plenty of primitive tasks for the primitive to do. But as these wretched tasks now begin to wither away, we are forced to examine, as we never have before, the meaning, far beyond the pay envelope and time clock, of how a human life is lived unexposed to knowledge, without even simple, practical, marketable skills. How do people get that way? Why do they stay that way? How can they become different?

 Is "primitive" too harsh a word? We are speaking of people who cannot read—millions of them. People to whom the thought of leaving a coal-mining town or a farm village is as fearful as floating blind in space. Old people who have performed simple manual tasks all their lives and are fearful of suddenly having to learn a slightly more complicated one. Young people convinced at the ages of six, ten, fifteen, that school is a prison that must be escaped at the earliest opportunity. People imprisoned in dark skins and by foreign tongues, so effectively locked out of the life we like to think of as civilization that aspiring to it seems a pointless game.

These, in the main, are what we call the chronically unemployed. These are the Americans whose long-suffering toil has recently been made unprofitable by automation, and whom we must bring into focus, the better to know what we're talking about when we speak of the chronically unemployed.

3

the new importance of don jones

Before meeting someone chronically unemployed—a man out of a job for fifteen weeks, six months, perhaps year after year—and considering what might be done about him, let's get to know more about the man we often think he is, and what is already being done about him. When we think of robots pushing workers aside, we think of factories, big noisy factories in great industrial regions. Like automobile factories in Michigan.

During World War II, when Donald Ray Jones was attending Eastern High School in Lansing, Michigan, hopeful men in Washington were proclaiming that we had embarked upon the Century of the Common Man. The man Don Jones has grown up to be is surely just the man they had been talking about in Washington.

45

Don Jones, is thirty-four, slim, strong, medium height, honest as gold, glad to work overtime to sweeten the family budget. Early each morning he checks the beds where his six children lie asleep, kisses his wife Jeanne, picks up a metal lunchbox, leaves his plain, shingled house in a street of plain, shingled houses, climbs into a station wagon that has already delivered many more miles than it has yet to give, and drives into the morning stream of factory-bound cars. Even the plainness of his name, Don Jones, seems designed to blend him into a mass image, as though he were a fictitious symbol. But I have talked at length with Don and Jeanne Jones, visited their shingled house in Lansing, played with their children. They are quite real.

About two years ago Don Jones, whose century they said it would be, learned with fearful suddenness that history had turned against him. After fifteen years of steady work—of taking his pick of employers—he was out in the street, unwanted. Men who performed unskilled tasks with their hands and simple tools were becoming useless. Almost anything an unskilled man could do, a machine could do better. It is a terrible thing to have one personnel man after another, week after week, month after month, look you up and down and say, "If we were hiring unskilled, you're the kind of man we'd hire. But sorry, that's not what we need."

You'd think a depression was on. But the smokestacks were smoking, the wheels whirring, the loading platforms loading, the dollars flying about like fresh-fallen leaves. Even the hiring offices were hiring. Want-ad columns were long ribbons of vacant jobs—from mechanics, machinists, and secretaries to computer programers, draftsmen, engineers, and scientists. The sarcastic old saw had finally been turned around: What counted was no longer *who* you knew but *what* you knew. To make a living, a fellow had to *know* something, have a skill. Like millions of Americans, Don Jones was unprepared for that new requirement.

In 1962 the federal government declared a limited war on lack of skill. At President John F. Kennedy's request, Congress began putting up $435 million in annual stages to help teach new skills to a million workers in three years. A few states—Michigan among them—didn't even wait for the federal money. They launched "pilot projects" so they would learn as quickly as possible the problems and promise of training workers to do jobs that machines don't do. Don Jones enrolled in Michigan's first class to train machine-tool operators. If he could begin to change in an 18-week course from a laborer to an artisan, from a performer of drudgery to an exerciser of judgment, from a collector of unemployment insurance to a secure taxpayer, then perhaps so could millions of others. He was an early test case, a kind of guinea pig. A new importance had come to Don Jones.

"I don't know where to begin putting you for training," a puzzled employment counselor told him, looking over the results of Don's aptitude tests. "You qualify for *everything.*" In general intelligence, numerical and manual aptitudes, Don rated high; in space and perspective comprehension, extraordinary. His results showed an aptitude for eighteen skilled occupations, but he had a useful, working knowledge of none.

What causes a man to reach his thirties without having acquired a salable expertness? Shiftlessness? In some cases, undoubtedly. Slowness of mind? In many cases, unquestionably. But an enormous number of unskilled men, such as Don Jones, are certainly not lazy or slow-minded. As sons of factory workers, miners, small farmers, they had learned from the hard lives of their fathers in earlier days that the important thing for making out in this world is not skill but job security. Only recently have the two words—skill and security—become tightly linked.

"I pictured my life pretty much like my dad's," Don told me across his kitchen table. "Dad worked at Reo Motors when I was born and he's at the same job today, checking out tools at the tool crib. No skill, but it's steady. If any part of the shop is working, the toolroom has to work, even in a depression. So I guess I grew up with the idea of a steady income like he had, never thinking much about getting rich—nor about being out of a job either."

As a boy, true, Don delighted in the romance of machines, the art of figuring. In high school he studied mechanical drawing and sometimes envisioned himself seated at a drawing board somewhere in a large sunlit room blue-printing important mechanisms. "When you get out of high school," Don observed, "you feel pretty important. You got that piece of paper that says you're educated and your head's still filled with all the answers you gave on the exams. You think you really know something. Then everywhere you go they ask, 'What experience do you have?' "

Don's only experience was working in a supermarket after school and on Saturdays for more than two years. So he did what seemed the natural thing. He stayed there full time. Like his father's job, the work was certainly steady; after all people had to eat. But after a couple of years Don had an operation. He was forbidden to lift cartons and he did the obvious thing for any unskilled youth in a city in Michigan. He went to work in an automobile factory.

At Lansing's huge Fisher Body works, Don was stationed beneath an awesome, clanking, endless beltline from which dangled an endless file of automobile shells, advancing upon him like a slow march of great skulls. As they came relentlessly, one upon another, each worker improved each passing shell with a single embellishment of a finished auto. Don's job was to install a panel that contained an ash tray and an armrest. "I learned the job in an hour. You had to know which tool to pick up, where to drill a hole and install the stuff. A little coordination was the whole thing."

In this repetitive, mindless task Don was useful to Fisher Body for two years, every few seconds picking up the same tool, drilling the same hole, installing the same panel. The pay was not high—about $1.75 an hour—but the station in life was honorable. As an auto worker, Don was the working man who did the things that needed doing, the man none of us could do without.

Layoffs were annoying but they were short (two or three days each) and rare (only three in two years). During the third of these layoffs, Don quit, taking a slightly better-paying job where his dad worked at Reo Motors, repetitively mounting a never-ending supply of wheels on a never-ending parade of army trucks. "Two dollars an hour," says Don, "was pretty good money compared to my first job at the supermarket. I felt pretty big again, just like when I graduated from high school."

It was an important time for Don to be feeling big, confident, secure. At a dance one night, Don had met Mary Jeanne Pohl, a doctor's receptionist. She too was confident and secure in a soft, wistful way. In three months Don and Jeanne were married and living in a house trailer that had been Don's bachelor home.

"My parents were skeptical about that trailer," says Jeanne, "but we were in love and it seemed fun. A year later, Susie—she's our ten-year-old—was on her way. I didn't cherish the idea of having a baby in a trailer. The floors were too cold."

They sold the trailer and put the money down toward a $7,000, two-bedroom house. In two years Chris was born, and two years later the first pair of twins, Kathy and Kevin. Now the children numbered four. The Joneses sold their house and bought another two-bedroomer that could be expanded. Don would add rooms first chance he got— maybe next summer.

One day in 1954 the huge, clanking beltline of trucks at Reo Motors stopped dead. A massive layoff virtually emptied the plant of its workers. This calamity in the lives of thousands had nothing to do with automation. Not even with a business recession. The plant, fully engaged in fulfilling its army contract, was suddenly told by the government, "No more trucks." Its contract had run out; there was to be no renewal. All over Michigan, automotive plants were reeling under the sudden realization that the big money in warfare had stopped riding on wheels and was soaring with missiles. The money had flown to Florida, California, Texas, St. Louis. (Later the much-publicized, disemployed workers of Republic Aviation, a conventional aircraft plant on Long Island, suffered the blow of the same unhappy truth.)

The biggest immediate trigger of unemployment in Michigan in recent years has been the very thing we rely upon for artificial prosperity: armament contracts, which begin like exploding fireworks and end abruptly like violent death. The other important cause of automotive unemployment, aside from temporary dips in consumer car sales, was a trend toward decentralizing the final assembly of cars. Assembly plants were set up in the East, West, and South, chiefly to save costs in shipping finished cars to market. Employment in auto plants has since fully recovered; the industry is booming. Early in 1964, Detroit unemployment was below 4 per cent, a rate far lower than the national one. Yet if almost anyone is asked why employment in the auto industry had come upon such hard times, the reply is almost always an unsure shrug and the suggestion, "Automation, I guess."

As the Reo Motors plant slowly converted to civilian production, a few workers trickled back to their jobs. But Don didn't wait to be called. The talk of automation had made him uneasy. True he had not heard of anyone in any auto plant being fired to make room for a machine. But what if they just put in machines during a layoff—say, to do the machinelike task of mounting a wheel on a passing truck, as Don had been doing—and then never called the men back to work? Don decided to take no chances. He applied for a job driving for the City Bus Company and got it—just like that. The wage rate was only $1.75 an hour but, with overtime, Don brought home $100 to $125 a week. Now he had real security, just like at the supermarket or the tool crib. After all, a city *had* to have buses.

But that last layoff—all those workers caught in it, many still out of jobs—still worried him. Sometimes he wished he could rely on something he knew, instead of circumstances he could in no way control. He thought of how much he'd liked mechanical drawing in high school, but that was many years ago. If only he could go into a small business of his own. . . . Don signed up for a correspondence course in electronics and T V repair.

"I couldn't learn about T V just from reading," he says today. "Every time I learned that something works a certain way I wanted to ask why, but I had no one to ask. I guess I'm too inquisitive. I always want to know why. I thought of going to Chicago and attending the school in person. But that would mean uprooting the kids. It seemed impossible."

"Anyhow," says Jeanne, "Don isn't really the type to be his own boss. He's got discipline for lots of things, but not the kind a man in business needs. If Don can put something off, he will."

Don nods regretful agreement.

His vague ambitions soon were obliterated by a stark reality. Their infant twins, Kevin and Kathy, both developed pneumonia. During one whole terrible week in oxygen tents the babies' lives were teetering, hour by hour. After the enormous relief of the twins' recovery, Don and Jeanne were left with the financial aftermath, $400 in medical bills not covered by insurance. They were more grateful than ever for the security of Don's bus-driving job.

But in 1959, with Don not alerted by so much as a whispered rumor, the bus company went broke. Still, Don was not in real trouble. His good five-year record as a bus driver got him a job for the asking as a driver of a transport truck delivering new cars to distant places. Jeanne didn't like it. Don would sometimes be gone for days at a time. He was paid by mileage so they could never plan on how much he'd bring home. She privately wished he'd quit. He'd find another good job. After all, Don had never really been unemployed in his life.

In June 1961, Don's truck was barreling down a highway at Hammond, Ontario. Not far ahead of him, the brake lights of another truck flashed on. Don's foot instinctively moved for his brake pedal and pressed. Nothing happened. As Don tells it, the brakes betrayed him until a split second before the trucks collided, when the brakes took hold. There was no way he could prove they had temporarily failed. His truck was a total loss, yet miraculously Don suffered only a cracked ear piece in his eyeglasses. The accident was the first Don had had in hundreds of thousands of miles of professional driving.

When he returned to Lansing, Don was given a pay check, a two-year safe driving award, and a pink slip. He was fired.

Only a few weeks earlier the Jones's second pair of twins had been born, but Don was unworried. A suburban bus company had taken over the old city bus routes. Don applied there. All the jobs were taken. The Reo plant had been sold to White Motor Company. Don applied there. No openings—except for men of skill. He went to other car-hauling and trucking outfits, even to the supermarket where he had worked before he was married. For the first time in his life—at the age of thirty-two—everywhere he went the word was "no."

Why? Business wasn't that bad. No one was saying Don was too old. Why was everybody saying "no"?

High-placed men were puzzling over the same question in Washington. The economy was active and healthy, yet almost five million workers were jobless. As the population grew, the number of people with jobs kept going up. But the number of people *without* jobs wouldn't go down.

Why? The ready answer was the reliable scapegoat, "automation." Robots were invading the factories and heaving men out. But as soon as one looked for evidence— which few thought it necessary to do—one began to wonder. Virtually none of the unemployed, except coal miners and farmers, had been directly displaced by machines. They had lost their jobs for less noteworthy reasons: a seasonal layoff, a small company gone out of business, a factory moved to another state, a government contract completed. But when they looked for new jobs, these people discovered that work was harder than usual to find. Many stayed unemployed.

Worried economists began to ask: who are these people who stay unemployed in the midst of prosperity? They were found to include large numbers of young people with neither high school diplomas nor significant work experience, older people approaching retirement age, Negroes in both city and country, and all sorts of people in regions that were economically depressed. Overwhelmingly these people had one characteristic in common. They were unskilled.

The service an unskilled man offers for sale is drudgery. This service, lowest in the scale of human capabilities, is the very one that man has sought to delegate to machines. Indeed, machines make men busier than they were before —one marvelous machine, the computer, has made possible the creation of a vast new industry, aerospace, employing hundreds of thousands—but these new jobs often require more education and training than men like Don Jones were prepared to offer.

Don Jones had lost his job in June. In July he was still filling out dreary applications, still hearing that dreaded word "no."

"I began to realize," says Jeanne, "that we might have to hold out till September. Often the summer is a quiet time for jobs. When we got into October and November, frankly I began to worry about what kind of Christmas the kids would have."

"At first I was more disgusted than scared," Don told me. "I knew I'd get a job, but it just wouldn't come. After working steady all those years we had some savings. Also I was collecting unemployment insurance of $55 a week. We had to cut corners now and Jeanne knew how to cut them. She baked all our bread, rolls, and doughnuts, the way she'd learned to do as a girl on a farm. The kids ate a whole lot more cereal than usual.

"I got pretty skilled at making a good product out of government-surplus powdered milk. We got lots of it free. The carton said to put four parts of water to one part of powder. I mixed two parts of warm water to one part powder, then threw in another two parts of ice cubes and cold water. That quick chill takes away the sticky, sweet taste that people object to in powdered milk. I found it just as good as milk from a carton.

"To keep busy at home I began digging a basement. That worked off a lot of tension. I learned that if you use a small enough shovel and plan a big enough basement, you can get a lot of idle time off your hands."

Meanwhile state employment officials were digging into another problem. If so many men needed jobs and so many jobs needed men, could men be trained to fit the jobs? A survey of Lansing employers revealed probable vacancies for sixty men trained in blueprint reading and use of precision machines: lathes, milling machines, grinders, shapers, drill presses, fine measuring gauges, and hardness testers. A man with such training could use it in almost any industry. He was not threatened by automation; in fact, he was more in demand because of it.

"One day in December," Jeanne recalls, "Don came home from the unemployment office and told me he was qualified to take this course if he wanted it. He'd keep getting his $55 a week, but he couldn't take a job for eighteen weeks. I told Don I'd find a job evenings to see him through. I was for it right away. What a blessing if Don could have a skill."

"I had already told them yes without hesitation," Don

says. "Then I began to have second thoughts. Eighteen weeks seemed so long. Maybe I'd find a job in that time. But the employment counselor kept saying words like 'skill' and 'maybe steady work.' After being out of a job so long, words like that have a pretty good sound."

Almost immediately Jeanne found an evening job at the switchboard of a nearby hospital.

In his new life as a student at Lansing Community College, where his classes were held, Don was surprised at how much mathematics and drafting a fellow needed to know just to equip him to learn one of the less advanced industrial skills. (A machine operator is far less skilled than, say, a machinist, which requires a four-year apprenticeship.) It gave him a new respect for the value of basic schooling; he'd have been lost without it.

In fact, a few of his fellow students did get lost. School preparation was not what they lacked; all were graduates of high school. What held them back, Don feels, was a lack of really caring about their own futures, feeling they could affect the course of their lives.

"Some of these fellows were pretty young, say, eighteen to twenty-one," says Don. "Here we were in a college, but these fellows never got out of high school—in their attitude, I mean. They didn't have a wife and six kids. Maybe a wife and no kids, maybe just six girl friends. They didn't have the same sense of urgency. This seems to make a lot of difference in how well you learn."

"We found that part of the training," said Frederick A. Hanses, manager of Lansing's state employment-service office, "has to be a changing of attitudes, introducing ideas on how to study, how to organize your thoughts, how to behave in groups. The first few days some of the fellows, especially the younger ones, were so undisciplined and disoriented from businesslike ways that during breaks they'd be out in the school hallway pitching pennies. A few had to be taken aside and tipped off. But in about the fourth week, the problem boys seemed surprisingly more interested and disciplined. They seemed to have a feeling, maybe for the first time in their lives, that they were headed somewhere."

"Some of these younger ones," says Frank C. Florey, the shop teacher and an enthusiastic educator, "would let their interests wander so easily. A ten-minute break comes, they take fifteen or twenty, apologize, then later do the same thing. I'm convinced that one of the basic reasons for some of these fellows lacking ambition and direction is that they had bad schoolteachers in their earliest grades. First- to third-grade teachers are the ones who shape learning attitudes. They should be the most carefully chosen, maybe the highest paid.

"The serious fellows here go through a three-hour class, sometimes take no break at all. They want to use every moment. I had one fellow who had a good factory inspection job, but it was a treadmill, leading nowhere. He confided to me that he arranged to get laid off so he'd be eligible for this course. A fellow like that is really here for business. He's sacrificing everything in his present for the sake of his future."

Don Jones was one of the serious students. At a graduation ceremony, attended by a representative of the Governor, Don was handed a certificate with the typed word "Outstanding." At first, he assumed all the certificates said that. Then he saw that the certificate of the man on one side of him said "Satisfactory," the man on the other side, "Satisfied minimum requirements."

Better still, Don already had been hired for a job. The following Monday he would put in his first day of gainful employment in nine months. For several days, as the course was ending, employers had come scouting for likely prospects among the students. Some students were jolted by the low pay they were offered—about $1.50 an hour. But every one of them got a job.

"I was disappointed, too," says Don, "but at least employers were recognizing that the course had taught us something. Doors were open to us. Somebody wanted to talk to us instead of looking over our applications and throwing them away. A lot of the boys overrated what an 18-week course could do for them. They expected to become skilled machinists at $2.50 an hour overnight. I'll admit even I was drawn into their optimism. You finish eighteen weeks times forty hours and you think you know something. You go to work at a bench next to a man who's been there seventeen years. You find out what's new to you is old to him. He's got more tricks than you ever dreamed of."

Don was hired—at $1.75 an hour to start—by the Industrial Welding Company. The company repairs broken parts of heavy machinery. Don, applying his knowledge of mechanical drawing and machining, measures and sketches the part to be repaired so it may be restored precisely to its original dimensions within thousandths of an inch. If he makes an error, the whole job may be bungled. With steadily scheduled overtime, Don has been earning $112 a week.

"That training program," says Wilson E. Campbell, Jr., Don's employer, "at least equips a man to come in the front door and start learning on the job. In a year a good man can start being of real value. He might be a journeyman in four years. Once a man starts learning, he becomes very important. Men who know machinery are hard to find. When we lose a good man it's a major problem."

Soon after Don began his new job he was back at

Lansing Community College taking a course in welding two nights a week. His employer pays half the tuition.

"That machine operator's course," says Don, "got me back in the swing of study. After welding I want to take some more math. I didn't know I could have been studying these things all along. I used to talk to a friend at the trucking company. We used to say how bad it was there are no trade courses an adult can take. Then I found out Lansing Community College has almost everything. After welding and math, what I'd really like to do is take some English. In high school I was always poor in spelling and reading. Those are the keys to education. If I got more confidence in my reading, I could go out and learn most anything. I may as well start now while I'm in the swing of learning."

When I asked Don and Jeanne if they were fearful of trouble yet to be caused by automation, they looked genuinely surprised.

"You can't spend your life being afraid of change," said Don. "This used to be farming country around here, but now it's factory country. Now that new machines are doing what people in the factory used to do, we've got to learn to run machines that can't run themselves. That's why I took that course."

So after nine months of dislocation—the penalty to himself and to society for insufficient training—Don Jones was restored to productivity, self-reliance, self-respect. Nine months of uselessness is painfully long to anyone who endures it. Yet it was short enough to be written off under the phrase, "All's well that ends well." Don has demonstrated to himself—and perhaps has helped demonstrate to others—the new and not unhappy fact of life in an era of automation: the simple secret to security is to keep learning.

But if the secret is that simple, why can't all the unemployed do as Don Jones has done? Why are some people lost among the melancholy statistics of the "chronically" unemployed?

Don Jones, untrained as he was, had acquired knowledge to build on. He had a diploma of a good American high school. He was a man of unimaginable learning compared to millions of Americans who are so uneducated, so poor, so removed from the mainstream of American life, they are, in a sense, living in another country.

4

illiteracy: the key to poverty

There is a man in Chicago who dares to think he has discovered the biggest cause of American poverty and how his city can begin to get rid of it. In fact, how any city can begin to get rid of it. His method—and this is not a flippancy—is as simple as teaching the A B Cs.

Raymond H. Hilliard, Director of Public Aid for Cook County, Illinois, recently was surprised to learn, after a long career of studying poverty, that most people who are extremely poor have in common a single, secret, crippling trait: they are virtually illiterate. He soon made other surprising discoveries. Impoverished illiterates and near-illiterates, no matter what their age, can be taught to read and write at insignificant cost ($5.50 a month), often in only a few months, and many can be made not only employable but employed. Perhaps most important of all, their education often leads to lifting the school interest and grades of their children.

"This," says Hilliard, "is the most hopeful thing I've ever had hold of."

To appreciate the seeming hopelessness against which Hilliard pits his hope, one must be willing to know how many Americans are poor and how poor they are. Not the underpaid, $1.25-an-hour minimum-wage poor, but the empty-pocket poor. If you take all the tens of millions of miserably rewarded sharecroppers and scavengers, mopslingers and laundry sorters, and even the jobseekers and their wives and kids who must make do on skimpy unemployment compensation checks, and *count them among the rich,* you still have seven and a half million souls who are *poor.* More than the combined populations of Los Angeles, Chicago, Pittsburgh, and Boston. Those are the Americans who live by the grace of public welfare. Their parents were poor and, unless something extraordinary is done rapidly, most of their kids will be poor. For the modern variety of "hard core" poverty has something in common with the elegance and security of established wealth. It is inherited.

One man who rose in a few months from hopelessness to hope is Sam Frost, a fifty-four-year old Negro ex-laborer with mighty shoulders and a stony, solemn, awesomely proud jaw. Frost (I have changed his name, but not his story) has fourteen children, the oldest still in school. In 1959, after a thirty-four-year history of steady employment, he was out of a job and could not for the life of him find a new one. Uneasiness turned to fear, then to horrible feelings of uselessness. Backaches and abdominal pains stabbed at him. These are the common occupational diseases of the unemployed; they seem to vanish only under the miracle drug of opportunity. Soon Frost reached the end of a downhill path: he and his large family landed on relief.

Two years ago Frost, like thousands of Chicagoans on relief, was given a test in the "three Rs." Like many others, he failed to show the formal learning of even a fifth-grade child. Soon he was "requested" to go to school two nights a week and do lots of homework in between (anyone refusing would forfeit his relief checks, but almost everyone went gladly). In a year and a half, Frost, an eager student, progressed from a near-illiterate to a possessor of an eighth-grade certificate—and more. His teacher, who volunteered to coach the student after classes, feels that Frost is almost ready to take an achievement exam for a full-fledged high-school diploma.

That still is not the most remarkable of Frost's accomplishments. Shell Oil Company admitted him to training as a gas-station attendant and taught him how to fill out a shift foreman's report, an intricate procedure for balancing all merchandise sold against money taken in. Frost mastered it better than some experienced foremen. Soon several station owners jointly hired Frost to circulate from station to station, combining the figures from shifts into daily round-the-clock reports, and finally into monthly reports. Also, he coaches station managers in better methods of record keeping. After more than five decades of ignorance, all this happened to Sam Frost in less than two years.

Now Milwaukee, Baltimore, Newark, and other cities are sending relief recipients to school. Like Chicago, they are teaching illiterates to read and write, others to qualify for grammar-school, even high-school, diplomas. These cities don't expect to find a Sam Frost behind every relief check. But they are convinced that only the thin walls of elementary schooling separate many good men from productive use of their native intelligence.

But is that intelligence really there to be developed and tapped? Anyone able to read these words will find it hard —almost impossible—to imagine the native cleverness one must have to make his way through a wordy world when he doesn't know how to read or write. In the way a blind man "sees" with his ears and fingers, or a deaf man "hears" by staring at lips, the illiterate must "read" his way around, not knowing one printed symbol from another.

Andrew Timmons had developed that special kind of cleverness. Standing near the entrance of the public housing project in Chicago where he lives with his wife and seven children, I pointed to a small wooden sign stuck into the dirt. It said, HELP US KEEP OUR LAWN BEAUTIFUL. I asked, "What does that sign say?" He replied confidently, "It says, 'Stay off the grass.'" I asked how he knew that. He said, "I just know that's what those signs always say."

At thirty-seven, Timmons (that is not his real name) distinguishes one street from another by its houses, not its street signs. When he once had a job downtown as a car washer—the only job he has found in the past nine years— he was able to find his way home on the Cottage Grove bus because he knows it is number 4. "I can read numbers," he assured me. When his wife sends him out for a can of tomato soup (which has only words on the label), he never brings home vegetable soup by mistake. He shops in the kind of grocery store where you ask for things, not where the customer selects from the shelf. Food is more costly there, but what can he do? Also, he has learned the ceremonial lies of the illiterate. Every culture has its ceremonial lies. Like the educated suburbanite who serves the best Scotch so his guests won't know he's broke, Timmons sometimes tucks a newspaper under his arm so his neighbors won't suspect he can't read. When people who work at desks give him papers to fill out (sometimes job applications), he says, "I just got my hands dirty. Could you put this in your typewriter and I'll tell you the answers?"

Timmons cannot, however, decipher a warning that says "Poison," a movie marquee, a big newspaper headline—or the tiny letters on newspapers' back pages that say "Help Wanted." He would be unable to compete for a job in a big, wordy city even if he knew where to find one. Timmons, his wife, and his seven children are on relief, all of them supported by his fellow citizens who *do* know how to read and write.

Why didn't Andrew Timmons—and the rest of the ignorant poor—learn when they had the chance? The fact is that while other children were going to school, Timmons, a native citizen of the land of free education and equal opportunity, was not given the chance to go.

"Where I was raised," he told me (he had grown up in Jasper County, Mississippi), "hardly none of the kids ever went to school a day. Nobody from the school made you go. My grandfather—he raised me 'cause my mother died when I was seven—figured going to school wouldn't help me pick cotton any better, so why go? I hardly ever thought a thing about it till I was about fourteen and saw some kids in a store looking at magazines and things and I wished I could do some of that. But it was too late."

Some did have the exceptional strength to defy such disadvantages, but even then defeat was almost inevitable. One of Timmons's housing-project neighbors—also on relief—is a spunky woman in her fifties. I'll call her

Maybelle Masters. Growing up in Shelburne, Mississippi,
she became determined not to mature into an ignorant,
helpless adult. At fifteen, she enrolled in the first grade.

"Walking four miles in the mud was the only way to get
to school," she told me. "Lots of kids didn't go because
they didn't have the right kind of high-top boots. On rainy
days, the school would be closed because the rain would
come down through the roof."

At the age of twenty—a fifth-grader—Maybelle got
married and quit school. According to the U. S. Census, she
is literate because she reported attending school for five
years, the minimum standard for "functional literacy." Yet
she cannot read and write.

Why not? Didn't she try hard enough?

"When they ask me how long I went," says Mrs. Masters, "I say five years, but the truth is I didn't go even
eighteen months. School was only open from January to
April. Sometimes the cotton wasn't all picked in January,
so you couldn't start school till the work was done. In April
the planting started. You stopped going to school when the
work started in the fields. So maybe I went two months a
year, maybe three."

Five "years" of schooling left her virtually as uneducated as Andrew Timmons who had had none.

Every large city is loaded down with Andrew
Timmonses, their burdened, bewildered women, and their
ragged, benighted children, the inheritors of what Hilliard
calls "infectious ignorance." Chicago is typical with 270,-
000 on relief. Some are southern Appalachian mountaineers (sometimes said to be the only white Anglo-
Saxon Protestants who, as a class, are victims of discrimination and deprivation). Some are Puerto Ricans,
Mexicans, American Indians. But overwhelmingly they are

Negroes who come from farms of the Deep South or whose parents did.

Much as America enjoys regarding itself as a nation of universal education, we have known the image is not entirely genuine. The 1960 Census tells us that eight million adults over twenty-five—one out of every dozen— attended school less than five years, thus are defined as "functionally illiterate." That figure strikes most people as dismayingly large. But the statistic is far smaller than the truth. Selective Service officials, for example, reject 22 per cent of draft registrants for failing a simple mental test; in Southern states the percentage of failures varies from 35 up to 56. They aren't deliberate flunkers; the test is mined with devices for trapping malingerers. Testing officers say that the young men fail mainly because they can't read the questions.

In Oklahoma City, a meat packer and two unions agreed jointly to retrain 170 workers displaced by new machines. The publicized calamity of automation in the lives of packinghouse workers in Oklahoma City, Omaha, and Chicago was one of the first national alarms that deepened our latest dread of machines. The dread grew deeper when word got about that the retraining programs were not very successful. But hardly anybody publicized why. The Oklahoma City retrainers found 110—or 65 per cent—of the workers too uneducated "to show promise of benefiting from training." More bluntly, the workers couldn't pass qualifying tests for the courses because they couldn't read and do simple figuring. In Michigan, where Don Jones's life had been changed by learning a skill, a group of 761 unemployed were tested for retraining; 515—or 68 per cent—failed. In Chicago, 4,500 on relief were tested; 1,900 were unable to read the questions well enough to pass.

Those figures reveal the startling difference between a man like Don Jones and the "chronically unemployed." Jones was equipped with a basic education to make himself ready for the new kinds of jobs created by automation and the prosperity it brings. Illiterates are not. A large Chicago restaurant chain needed good help so badly it had to turn to Europe to recruit, yet in America 287 unemployed had to be tested to find 20 literate enough to train as cooks—reading recipes and the scribbled orders from waitresses. Hospitals, desperate for nurses, either registered or practical, have brought students from the Philippines, yet 500 unemployed American women had to be tested to find 30 literate enough for a class in practical nursing. In the recent past, a man became a janitor if he could qualify for nothing else. But today a janitor is no longer a mindless floorsweeper. He must operate cleaning machines of complexity, study a manual for making repairs. There are even training classes for janitors; in Washington, D. C., many applicants were turned down because, unable to read labels, they couldn't distinguish a box of detergent from rat poison.

Are new machines to blame? Are we to label these people "victims of automation"? Or shall we at last attribute their ignorance to the primitive world of preautomation, which has condemned so many people for so long to such drudgery as chopping cotton, and educating them for no more? Is automation victimizing them, or rescuing them? The new, humanizing demands of automation are changing illiteracy from an unfortunate—and often ignored—statistic to a serious national threat.

Hilliard, the Chicago welfare chief, started becoming aware of the secret, growing threat of illiteracy in January 1959. He was disturbed by a statistical chart on his desk and he called in his energetic, intensely inquiring research director, Deton J. Brooks, Jr. A recession had just ended. Employment was picking up. According to all past experience, the relief rolls, which had always reacted sensitively to ups and downs of business, should be declining. But they kept rising. Why?

Hilliard and Brooks decided on an intensive study of a large, crowded, poverty-stricken neighborhood called Woodlawn where 25 per cent of all households were on relief. One of their findings seemed to tower in significance above all others. According to the Census, 6.6 per cent of the relief recipients had five years of schooling or less. But standard tests in the three Rs revealed that measurements of literacy based on "years" in school are widely misleading. A startling 51 per cent of the able-bodied adults were found unable to read and write at a fifth-grade level. The remainder who tested higher were so little above functional illiteracy that the difference hardly mattered. Nearly all were too uneducated to get the simplest jobs in the modern labor market.

"Here then" said Hilliard, reporting his findings to a convention of welfare officials, "is the major cause of today's poverty. Here is the reason for the high cost of relief. Punishing these people for their poverty won't help, badgering them with investigations, violating their small rights of privacy, condemning them for alleged immorality, putting them in jail, calling them loafers and idlers and cheats and frauds, which few of them are, will avail nothing. . . . These only divert attention from real solutions."

As a real solution, Hilliard set about to teach fifty thousand relief recipients to read and write better. By December 1963 the eight thousand most urgently needing education were going to school, but money was lacking for the rest. The Chicago Board of Education began footing the entire cost, providing classrooms and paying regular school teachers $4.50 an hour for the two evenings each week that classes are held. To pay these costs, the Board of Education siphoned money that was earmarked for Americanizing the foreign-born. Later, Congress authorized the use of federal funds for teaching literacy to the unemployed.

The biggest initial problem, according to Hilliard, was arranging for baby sitters to free mothers for classes. If women's organizations were prepared to offer such help, he said, they would make a unique contribution to helping families rid themselves of poverty. But lacking such help, welfare caseworkers undertook the huge job of arranging mutual baby sitting among the student-mothers. Last summer, when classes were changed to daytime to save custodial costs in school buildings, the baby-sitting problem became so difficult many classes had to be cancelled.

Considering how many classes for teaching literacy to adults have been springing up around America, one would expect the techniques to be down to a science. In Yakima, Washington, the LARK (Literacy for Adults and Related Knowledge) Foundation has organized classes as far east as Michigan. In St. Louis the Adult Education Council has aggressively sought to educate illiterates. Indiana Central College started a course for teaching teachers of illiterates. Daily T V programs, one series produced in Philadelphia, another in Memphis, have been loaned to other cities in the hope that illiterates will tune in and learn to read. But everywhere, teachers are groping for effective teaching methods.

The absence of recognized teaching materials came as a shock to Robert L. Dixon, a junior-high-school teacher supervising some Chicago welfare classes. He recalls the first orientation meeting of several hundred teachers.

"Before you ask what textbooks you are to use," the speaker said, "let me tell you that we have none. We know that the Little Red Hen won't do for adults, but we don't know what *will* do. Your students are not like immigrants who want to learn to speak English. For most of your students English is the only language they know. This challenge is new. We will have to find our way by experimenting."

Dixon faced his first class, composed entirely of Negroes like himself, with uneasiness. His chief tools were a piece of chalk and a blackboard. His twenty students sat in the unfamiliar pose of poising pencils over notebooks. There were two women for each man. Young people outnumbered the elderly.

"First I wondered how much they knew about the world," he told me. "Next, I wondered how much they knew that I don't know. I had to keep reminding myself that they had rich experiences I know nothing about. One had been a paint mixer, one a drill-press operator, a few housewives and mothers, each with full lives, some longer than mine. I had to remind myself not to lump them together with a simple label like 'illiterate.'

"Then I began to wonder how much they thought I knew, what they imagined book learning really is. This made me wonder—and this was the most troubling of all— how much they expected of me."

His students came with uneasiness, too.

"I wondered," said Eddie O'Brien, a father of twelve, "how much education a man needed so he could get himself a job, and how long it would take. I was forty-two already and didn't have much time."

O'Brien took it as no joke when one night Mr. Dixon distributed play money and set up a shelf full of commodities for "sale." As pupils "bought" things, the teacher spun a line of talk, meanwhile shortchanging each of his customers. They were first embarrassed, then stunned as Mr. Dixon revealed the utterly simple ways in which slick salesmen fleece the uneducated.

These ways already had cost O'Brien his last job. For seven years he had worked for a baking company, stacking crackers as they came down automatic conveyors and sweeping crumbs from the floor. He took home $84 a week.

"I wanted to be like the rest of the people," O'Brien told me. "I bought a used car, some furniture we needed, a T V set, clothes for the kids. Those salesmen, they always kept telling me it wasn't hard, just a dollar down, a dollar a week. Before I knew it, I was caught in the trick bag."

The "trick bag" had many hidden pockets. If educated people are often swindled for overlooking the fine print, how easy to skin someone unable to read even the big print. One day a lawyer informed O'Brien he could be saved from his excess number of creditors only by claiming personal bankruptcy. The lawyer would gladly arrange this at a cost of $300. Payments would be easy: $100 down, $40 a month. When the fourth payment for the lawyer fell due, O'Brien was unable to pay it. Thus he forfeited $220 he had already paid, and the lawyer abandoned the case. O'Brien was undefended when his creditors descended on the baking company to claim slices of his wages. He was fired for "excessive wage assignments," a phrase well known in slum districts. Soon his family was on relief.

O'Brien's teacher, Mr. Dixon, includes in his instruction the essentials of how to be a good employee, such as the idea of "job loyalty." But the idea is hard to get across. When Eddie O'Brien needed his job most—to get out of the debt he was tricked into—he was fired for getting into debt. Nobody stood by him. When Andrew Timmons worked at his only job in nine years—at the car washer's—

his employer once hailed him from the steamy wash tunnel and sent him into the bitter cold of December to fetch coffee for the front office. Timmons caught a chill, developed pneumonia, and spent Christmas near death in a hospital. When he recovered, he found that another man had been given his job and the boss was "too busy" to talk things over. That's when Timmons began heading for the relief rolls.

"How does a man learn loyalty," Dixon asks, almost in futility, "when no one has ever been loyal to him? He doesn't see it and he can't even read about it. We expect him to know the importance of regular attendance at work. Yet all his life he's been told to come and told to go, on a day's notice or an hour's, always at the employer's convenience. He only knows what he has seen. And he hasn't seen much to support our lectures on the rewards of being a good employee."

Still the students come eager to learn. After the first embarrassment at being exposed to their friends as uneducated, many are seized with a desire to know how to spell their children's names. They recite the names to the teacher and become absorbed in the magical process of copying down the letters—sometimes the first meaningful syllables they have ever written in their lives. One woman, after only three months of tutelage, brought her teacher an elaborate chocolate cake. She carried it proudly and announced, "I got a book all about cooking and *read* how to make it."

Eddie O'Brien describes his sense of achievement differently: "I feel like a caged bird that all at once got out." His escape has indeed been dramatic, for he escaped into the comparatively exhilarating world of self-dependence and self-respect. O'Brien began averaging $450 a month driving a taxi. He is one of the most successful of almost five hundred drivers lifted from the literacy classes and relief rolls, and being trained for jobs by the Yellow Cab Company. Once they had demonstrated they could read street signs, they were taught Chicago's house-numbering system, the location of the city's seventy-eight most important buildings, and how to fill out trip reports. Also they were given special training in meeting the public —and how to buy sensibly on the installment plan.

Yellow Cab expects to train a thousand relief recipients, possibly more. Despite publicized unemployment, the company has constant trouble finding suitable men. After surveying its own employees, the company drew up a description of the man who seemed most likely to succeed at the wheel. He was middle-aged, had children, little formal education, was probably a Negro, and his last employment was as a laborer or packinghouse worker. These characteristics, the company learned, almost exactly described the able-bodied male on relief. They also described the man least likely to be aware of a shifting national pattern of jobs from the factory (such as packinghouses) to services (such as cab driving). He is the man most fearful of looking for a job different from the one he had before. Of the first 406 to be educated and lifted from the public's relief roll to Yellow Cab's payroll, 333 made a go of driving cabs. Of the remainder, many left for other, better jobs; a few entered military service. A handful were fired for careless driving.

Soon after the success was apparent, the Chicago Urban League brought the Yellow Cab story to the Shell Oil Company. Major oil companies have been troubled by a shortage of high-grade men as gas station attendants. Sales are lost by employees who don't seem to care, and the man who meets the customer can make or break the reputation of his company.

With trepidation, Shell undertook to train a group of men from the literacy classes. Strange things happened. In tests for spelling, for example, men continued to have trouble with words like "which," but racked up high scores in technical words like "detergency" and "differential." Company officials accepted this as a surprising sign that the men were burning late lamps to insure succeeding on their new jobs. It helped destroy company fears that "reliefers" were natural loafers. Still, the company was skeptical. Yet two months after the men went to work for neighborhood dealers, the company found that seven out of thirty-five had already been promoted to shift foremen, taking charge of men who had been on the job a year or more. Station owners reported that the new men were among their best employees. The training program is now permanent.

While the star trainee at Shell, Sam Frost, who became the roving bookkeeper, was working furiously to learn, an odd thing happened at home. His eighteen-year old son, a recent high-school dropout, began talking about going back to school; his grammar-school children headed for their homework whenever Daddy did.

This discovery was made in many families, some of which never had occasion to own a book, seldom a newspaper.

"Children do what their grown folks do," Mrs. Dorothy Slade told me, slightly awed by the behavior of her eight-year-old son. "Since I been going to school, it seems he just behaves better. I used to play solitaire and he'd want to take the cards to bed with him. I stopped playing because I don't think children should learn about cards. Now I pick up a book, and darn if he don't pick up one of his school-books. Now look and see what's happening to his marks."

Mrs. Slade showed me report cards for two years. The

previous year the child had earned an F (fair) in reading
and G (good) in arithmetic. This year's grades were E
(excellent) in both subjects.

The experience of Mrs. Slade and her son—duplicated
in many households I looked into—helps explain Raymond
Hilliard's enthusiasm for educating mothers, even though
many might not become self-supporting at jobs. These
mothers may slow the spread of "infectious ignorance."
Mrs. Slade's son has no father to model himself after; he
was born out of wedlock. The Woodlawn study revealed
that 84 per cent of able-bodied adults on relief are women,
most of them abandoned early in marriage. Hilliard's
research director, Deton Brooks, emphasizes:

"In a matriarchal structure, the women are transmitting
the culture. If the woman is illiterate, she transmits the
values, the images, of an illiterate's world. She can't do
otherwise. This is dangerous, extremely dangerous, for the
future of these children and the society that may soon have
to support them as illiterate adults."

Extending this reasoning, Hilliard is convinced that
literacy classes strike at the roots of broken homes. Hilliard
concludes:

"You can see a straight line operating from illiteracy to
illegitimacy. The American culture teaches all men—
including Negro men segregated from the main culture—
that a father's job is to be a provider. The man who had
been abandoned by his father and in turn abandons his
children is convinced he can never succeed as a good
American father. Where's his chance to provide? From the
day he takes his vows he knows he can't fulfill his function,
that his manhood has been taken away, that his marriage is
doomed, and the insecurity of his woman has begun.

"Instead of heaping more contempt on this man, let's
look for ways that will let him stay at home. Let's give him

at least the meagerest education to help him find a decent job at a decent wage, and give him some assurance that he won't be the first one fired because of his color. Then you'll start to see a downslide in the illegitimacy rate. That's how you can extend the possible results—maybe very early results—of something as simple as teaching the A B Cs."

The unhappy, unproductive survival of an illiterate primitive with a large family costs an American city $300, $400, sometimes $500 a month. Perhaps it is sinful to take measure of this human misery in dollars, but that is the original sin in which the misery was born. For the uselessness of these people did not begin when the machines came. It was ordained when their native states—Mississippi, Kentucky, Alabama, Arkansas, and all the rest—saw no purpose in spending even $200 *a year* to school their cotton pickers and squirrel hunters.

Now that this sin against humanity has at last received overnight recognition, Americans would like to make overnight repentance, quickly, painlessly. But there is no way. In denying education, we have taught lessons of aimlessness, futility, inferiority and self-hatred. We have taught these lessons well; they will not quickly or easily be unlearned.

Occasionally a Sam Frost will make the effort against ignorance look like victory. The success of the Yellow Cab and Shell Oil experiments give us the flushed hope that perhaps there is some kind of overnight repentance.

But then one visits the literacy classes. The truth he must face is that great numbers of lost souls are hopeless in trying to cram the alphabet into their aging heads. They go to classes because they are told to go. They sit with pencils poised because that's what others do. Perhaps they even engage in some fumbling inner struggle with them-

selves to try to study. But it is too late. In darkness they
have lived; in darkness they will remain for what time
they may have remaining.

What is to be done?

"You can't just ignore these people," goes a familiar
argument. "Your long range optimism is all very well, but
these people are out of work *now*. Your new machines may
create new jobs, all right, but not for the unskilled and
illiterate. What do you propose to do for *them—now?*"

What must be done is obvious. They must continue to
be kept, as they are today, and have been for years, by
the society that misused them. But the question is for
how many generations must the chain of inherited dependence go on? When "liberals" reply with the facile demand that we "must take care of these people," are they
not condemning them, in the name of compassion, to a
continuation of the same dark, outcast lives to which "conservatives" often condemn them with contempt?

The chronically poor cannot be ignored, of course not.
But their condition of ignorance cannot be accepted as
static and unchangeable, either. Something indeed must
be done for them now.

Of all the "somethings" that have been proposed—a
moratorium on installing new machines; expansion of government make-work projects designed more to employ
than to build; and the latest one, rearranging our national
ethics to divorce the idea of income from the idea of work
—only one plan addresses itself to what the trouble really
is. If the trouble is ignorance, the solution must be education. All the rest is flailing of the arms that brings relief to
nothing except the troubled social conscience of the arm
flailer.

The education of illiterates and near-illiterates is not
only mandatory but comparatively cheap. The cost of

teaching one jobless man in Chicago for five years is smaller than his relief check for a single month. The schooling may provide his shortest, most practical route back to useful work. But the important thing is that the education is useful and a bargain *even if he doesn't learn.* For his simple acts of going to school, carrying home the first book he ever laid his hands on, clearing the kitchen table and licking his pencil to do homework, are, when exposed to the eyes of his slum-imprisoned children, the essential first acts in breaking the chain of dependence. These simple gestures are what may first reveal to a child that school-learning has some real connection with the real life of some real adult he knows.

Compelling as the need may be to help a man too ignorant to perform a job, the need is far more compelling to save his children from such crippling ignorance while they still may be saved.

5

not like other children

In thinking about automation, it has become a commonplace to think how terrible it is that nobody knows who tomorrow's unemployed will be.

But the terrible thing is that we know almost precisely who they will be and where they are today. One may walk into today's schoolhouses and pick out the eight-, ten-, twelve-year-olds who are undergoing intensive training for lives of uselessness and hopelessness. Yet no one seems equal to saving them from their seemingly inevitable fate. These children are massed together by the thousands, each a prisoner of the rest, in schools of the vast slums of our cities. If today's slum child has hope on the day of his enrollment in first grade of one day making something of himself, that hope is destroyed by the time he becomes a school dropout, which, according to the figures, he is reasonably sure of becoming.

The school dropout has become almost a glamour figure of our decade. We invest money, time, and talent in trying to help him find his way back to the mainstream of the society that drove him out. But we still know so little about his agonized relationship with his school. What is education like in a compulsory-attendance, tax-supported school that trains masses of pupils for mass unemployment?

When I began trying to find out what is really happening in these schools, I made the error—suggested by the very term "slum schools"—of setting out prepared to be appalled by the condition of schoolhouses.

That's the same error that almost everybody makes. The week I began, a committee of six congressmen had become upset by a growing educational failure in the schools of the nation's capital, as well as by rising racial tensions. They sensed something had to be done. What did they do? They went out to look at dilapidated schoolhouses, which were not hard to find.

In Pierce School, built in 1894 for 280 pupils, they found 400 enrolled in eight rooms, no provision for hot lunches, no auditorium, no health room, no library. Ceiling plaster drops on desks; windows are shaded by sheets of wrapping paper. The congressmen expressed shock.

I had no trouble finding schoolhouse squalor either. In New York, at Public School 103 I didn't get as far as the principal's office before suffering an assault of sickening fumes—piercing, pervasive odors of decayed plaster and stale urine, too impregnated in the ancient schoolhouse walls ever to be washed away.

Such conditions, of course, are shocking and deserve exposure. But also they are peculiarly comforting. They help strengthen a favorite American myth. The myth is that we can ride a bulldozer to higher national literacy merely by knocking down old, deteriorated classrooms and building glassy, gleaming new ones. But the reality is that schools in the central sections of our major cities are factories of failure, and the school buildings that house them have little to do with the matter. Whole school systems are surrendering on a mass scale in their struggle to educate the children of the impoverished, and blaming their failure on the victims—the children and their parents.

In brand new, gaily painted buildings as well as antiquated, shabby ones, the eyes of the children are dull, detached, uninterested, the faces of the teachers harassed and helpless. From open doors the most frequently heard sound is a teacher's "*Shhhhhhhh!*" Sometimes a desperate variation, "James, sit *down* and shut *up!*" In the streamlined teachers' lunchrooms of new buildings, shoptalk about pupils includes a high incidence of the word "dumb." Ask a teacher why the kids are so "dumb" and you hear, after a troubled shrug, "I try every way I know to teach them, but they don't *want* to learn. After all, *look at their I Qs.*"

That is the teacher's ultimate condemnation. One of the rules she memorized at teachers college is that an intelligence quotient describes the classroom potential of a child. If the number is low, the child is a goner, unteachable, "dumb."

Recently the idea has crystallized in the minds of a few people—a school superintendent here, a Ford Foundation official there, a professor of psychiatry here, a school social worker there—that the slum child is a child of another world. Our laws do not bind him, our standard middle-class ambitions do not inspire him, our I Qs do not measure him, and, most of all, his teacher is not reaching him. Rules she learned in teachers college clearly don't work in the slum school, but she clings to them, for no one has taught her different rules. Teachers in first to third grades feel the child slipping away. By the fourth grade he has fallen behind. By the eighth grade he may be as many as three years back, his mind closed, his behavior rebellious. By high-school age, he is more than likely a dropout, headed for chronic unemployment, disdaining the "outside" middle-class world that already disdains him, secretly contemptuous of himself, a waste of a human being. A failure.

The few people who are trying to understand this child have given him a name, not a satisfactory name, but a name: they call him "culturally deprived." What defines him is not an absence of money or nice clothes or good furniture or cars or food, although all these objects are relatively lacking. These children suffer from a poverty of experience. Perhaps their lives are rich with experiences their teachers know nothing about. But they are growing up unequipped to live in an urban, primarily middle-class, world of papers and pens, books and conversations, machines and desks and time clocks.

Their numbers are staggering. While in 1950 one child out of every ten in America's fourteen largest cities was "culturally deprived," by 1960 the figure had become an alarming *one out of three.* This is an estimate made for the Ford Foundation by a group of big-city school boards organized as the Great Cities School Improvement Studies. By 1970 one of every two big-city children is expected to be counted as "culturally deprived."

Their composition is like that of the Chicago illiterates on relief. In fact, it may be said that these are their children; children of coal miners and "branch water" farmers of the Southern Appalachian backwoods, driven to the cities when their land would no longer support an ever-growing population; children of Puerto Ricans, Mexicans, refugees from American Indian reservations. But mostly they are the children of Negroes. Chicago's elementary-school enrollment is 46 per cent Negro. Philadelphia's and Baltimore's are about the same. New York's is 27 per cent (Negroes and Puerto Ricans in Manhattan total 76 per cent). The percentage of Negro children in Washington public schools is a lopsided 85. These proportions are constantly, inexorably growing.

Ten years from now, when many of these children, like their parents, will be on relief, unemployable in a society demanding increased human skills, and when their children in even vaster numbers are failing to learn from their bewildered teachers, a congressman will rise, as many do every year, to protest that the cost of the dole is killing us. How, he will ask, can we dare mortgage our grandchildren by the cost of today's handouts? Yet so few men of responsibility are asking what investment may be made in today's classrooms—to change the architecture not only of walls but of lives—so millions of our young may be saved from defeat, economic uselessness, and spiritual hopelessness.

What investment can be made? This is what I tried to find out in talking to teacher after teacher, child after child, in school after school, city after city. The problems may not be as hopeless as they seem. But the problems are not what most of us think they are, either.

I met Tracy in a classroom in Milwaukee. Two years ago he came to Milwaukee from Mississippi, one unnoticed soul in the great migratory wave from declining Southern farmlands to Northern industrial cities. Tracy (that is not his real name) is twelve years old. When his mother brought him to enroll in the strange northern schoolhouse, he looked and acted "dumb": sullen, staring without focus when spoken to, responding to questions not in sentences but in monosyllabic grunts. He was given a standard intelligence test for "nonverbal" children, and scored a 66. That number confirmed, as almost any certified teacher will vow, that Tracy, like so many of his slum schoolmates, was a lost cause. The proof was in the pudding—at the age of ten he was unable to muddle through a first-grade reader.

Was he really that unteachable? Was it possible that his I Q, his manner, even the color of his skin, were a curtain hiding from his teachers an active, eager intelligence starved for experience to nourish on? By statistical accident, Tracy was chosen at random from among thousands for an experimental class of twenty children, one of seven such classes in Milwaukee subsidized by the Ford Foundation. His classmates' I Qs were like Tracy's: 73, 64, 81, 71, 77. Illiterates and near illiterates all. Some were old enough for junior high school, but all were classified as "first to fourth grade, ungraded."

In a year and a half, his teacher, Mrs. Marguerite Stangel, a stocky, stern-looking woman, ignoring Tracy's "unteachability," succeeded in teaching him. "A child does what's expected of him," she told me. "His teachers had convinced him he couldn't do anything. They convinced his mother. She told me, 'Teacher, I hope you can learn him. Nobody I ever saw could learn him.' Whenever I got him to learn something I'd make him write it on the board and I'd say, 'There, you did it.' He'd look astonished, as though to say, 'I didn't know it was that easy. I *did* it.' "

Mrs. Stangel led me to a bulletin board covered with papers of careful writing. Not just lists of words, nor even sentences, but poems—original poems—for Lincoln's

Birthday. I liked Tracy's best. Decorated by a neatly scissored silhouette of Lincoln, his poem read:

> Abraham Lincoln grew up to be a very nice man.
> He believed in freedom for every man.
> He went to a theater one fine night.
> And a half-crazy actor shot him at sight.

It was less than Shakespearean. But as the work of a child who a few months earlier couldn't read "Look, Dick, Look," it brought on a tremor of dreadful wonder at how many intelligences are buried and suffocating beneath a teacher's conclusion, buttressed by an I Q score, that a child is "dumb."

I called Tracy over. The class had already been let out but a few boys were still there doing chores. Mrs. Stangel told me they had not been ordered to stay; they just liked to. Tracy was lining up desks in precise military formation. His body was alive with boyish fidgeting, but his face dull. He would not focus his eyes on me.

"What are you going to do when you're all finished with school?" I asked.

"Go down the gym. Play basketball."

"I don't mean today," I said. "I mean when you're all finished going to school. What do you want to be when you grow up?"

He looked out the window, eyes unsteady and gently blinking. He said nothing. As I waited, he droned a note as though on the edge of a pronouncement, but no thought would come.

I had asked this question of dozens upon dozens of boys in slum schools—young white mountaineers and young Negroes. The mountain children often try for a few seconds to understand the odd question. Then their concentration would melt away. No words. The question was too far out. Young Negroes—say, six or seven years old —would usually produce an answer, and it was almost always the same:

"Baseball player."

"What team?"

"San Francisco Giants."

"What position?"

"Center field."

Everyone knows who plays there. Willie Mays.

"What if there's no job for you on a baseball team?"

"Be basketball player."

"What if all the teams have all the players they need? What if you get a job to do work? What kind of job would you get?"

Then the Negro child's mind, like the mountain boy's, strains for a moment and seems to go blank.

These, of course, were six-year-olds. But Tracy was twelve years old—almost old enough to drop out of school. He was old enough to know there can be only one Willie Mays. What other worthwhile ambitions remained? Like most twelve-year-olds I asked, Tracy grappled with the question wordlessly.

"What does your father do?" I asked.

"My father? When?"

"What does he do when he works?"

"Sometimes they call him. He—I guess he wash cars."

"All right. Now what kind of work do you want to do when you grow up?"

Now that he knew what I was getting at, he squinted thoughtfully, as though to take inventory of all the far-ranging occupations he could imagine. But none seemed to come to mind.

Mrs. Stangel came to my aid. "Did you ever see anybody working whose work you would like to do?"

After a strained silence, Tracy finally said, "Like to be the boss in a store."

"What kind of store?" I asked. The question confounded him again.

"A department store?" prodded Mrs. Stangel. Silence. His forehead began to sweat. I don't think he knew about department stores. Then he said, apparently reaching out as far as his worldly knowledge would take him:

"Grocery store."

"Why," I asked, "would you like to be a boss in a grocery store?"

His answer was ready and reasonable.

" 'Cause anything that was there you could get."

If he was stretching his imagination strenuously to understand the meaning of my questions, I had to stretch mine just as strenuously to get the meaning of his answers. It is difficult to comprehend the world of a child who has hardly ever seen a man of his color performing any task honored by society, except playing baseball or doing something musical. Adults in his world do not ask a child what he wants to be when he grows up. They do not generally talk about work. For the working day is when they are held in lowest esteem, by themselves as well as by others. Grown men of dark color, if not great stars like Willie Mays, are part-time car washers like Tracy's father. But hardly anything in between, as far as Tracy has ever seen. Ambition for a career is either unreasonable or untenable; a thought so unfruitful does not ordinarily come to mind.

In a classroom in a slum school in Chicago a conscientious white teacher proudly showed me some drawings made by her sixth-graders. Only one pictured a person. It was a remarkably skilled rendition of a boy, wearing a straw Huckleberry Finn hat, sucking a weed, fishing at a riverbank. The boy in the picture was white.

I looked around. Not a white child in the class. The teacher, sensing my unspoken question, handed me an elementary reader, a Dick and Jane story. "Do you see any children here," she asked quietly, "who aren't white? That boy has never seen a picture of a Negro child. At least not a real picture in a book. He already knows a colored child isn't good enough to be in a picture."

Does he ever see *any* Negro in a school reader?

"Yes," the teacher said. "When Dick and Jane go visit their grandmother in the country—which these children don't understand because grandmother lives with *them*— and they ride on a train to get there—these children have never ridden on a train—they are served by a Negro porter. The book isn't about children like them. It's a silly fairy tale about things they can't imagine. Why learn to read it? In fact, why learn to read?"

Because the books seem stupid, the children's negative response to them appears stupid. Other elements in the background of the slum child help complete a classical portrait, as described in standard teacher education, of stupidity.

"How can I teach them," I was asked by teacher after teacher, "when they have no attention span? They just *won't* concentrate."

Psychologists are beginning to discern that the slum child's inattention may be a high skill, the result of intensive training. When a child lives with eleven people in three rooms, separated by thin walls from other households of eleven people in three other rooms, smelling their cooking, sharing their toilets, knowing when the man is drunk next door and the baby awake downstairs—a child must *learn* to be inattentive to survive. His ears become skilled at not hearing, his eyes at not seeing.

Dr. Martin Deutsch, of the Institute for Developmental Studies, tells of a boy who seemed a social misfit. A school psychologist, moved to investigate, learned that the boy liked to lock himself in a closet. This had ominous Freudian implications, such as a need to withdraw to the dark comfort of the womb. To confuse the implications, however, the boy showed a predilection for a certain closet in which he could turn on an electric light. On investigating this deviation, the psychologist discovered that the boy —indeed a misfit among his peers—merely liked to read. He would go to all lengths to do so in quiet, including locking himself in a closet. This eccentricity had led his family and school to suspect that he was seriously out of his head.

Most teachers hardly suspect other forms of the slum child's poverty of—or differences in—experience. Dr. Deutsch's staff has found that kindergarten children often have not learned one color from another, except red and blue. No one has told them to wear the pink dress today or wondered aloud in their presence about the advisability of getting lavender draperies to go with the gray rug. They may be unaware of shapes—blocks, circles, squares, the idea of short and long. The teacher assumes a knowledge of these things. She often cannot conceive of a child's not knowing colors and shapes—except a very "dumb" child. One teacher, trying to teach reading through a story about a snowman, was baffled to learn that some children assumed a snowman is a man who shovels snow from city streets; they had *seen* one of those, but knew of no other kind. She later found that one of her children was sure a fire engine's purpose was to bring fire. No one had ever told him otherwise.

In fact, no one ever tells slum children much about anything. Conversation is not a highly developed art in their families. Suddenly the child, accustomed to learning through his senses, is obliged to sit still all day before a talkative teacher—she can talk for hours without stopping. Moreover, she seems to think the most important thing in the world is to make out printed words on a page. About half the children surveyed by Dr. Deutsch came from homes that did not possess a single book. Instead of bringing the middle-class teacher and the impoverished pupil closer together, words may only help to drive them apart, underlining the distance between their worlds.

The teacher of early grades may remain largely unaware that her pupils aren't following her. The fifth- and sixth-grade teachers find out with a jolt.

"Those are the grades," says Dr. Deutsch, "when learning depends more and more on abstractions: What is a nation? What happened in the past? Suddenly it's discovered these children are unprepared for skilled use of such basic abstract ideas as bigger and smaller, higher and lower, round and square. They are untrained in ideas that grow from numbers. A child may know that Yankee Stadium holds a large number of people, but doesn't know if that large number is closer to 100 or 100,000.

"He is comparatively unprepared to deal skillfully with the idea of time, the past, the future, planning, scheduling. The middle-class American notion of the value of time or the careful allotment of it appears to be comparatively absent in the culture of the slums, just as it is almost entirely absent in the life of certain Indian tribes. This is extremely difficult for most time-oriented Americans to grasp. Often a teacher interprets a child's disregard for time as a form of rebellion or stupidity, instead of a problem in cultural difference."

By the time the child is old enough to drop out of school, he is well insulated from other standard American values.

"It's hard for outsiders to understand," says Mrs. Zenobia Baxter, a school counselor in Chicago working with dropouts, "that for many of these children 'work' is only a word. They have never seen anyone work. If there's a man at home, there's a good chance he's unemployed. But in 50 per cent of these homes there is no man at the head of the house at all."

Mrs. Baxter organizes visits to offices and factories to demonstrate what people do when they work—how a knowledge of words and numbers helps them live better. She organizes trips to the Loop—Chicago's downtown district—for teenagers and parents who have never been there even though it is only thirty blocks from the heart of the slums. They never had occasion to go because they can't get jobs in Loop offices and do not feel welcome in the stores.

After these visits, Mrs. Baxter leads dropouts in discussing what wages are, what one must do to get them, how one's life is improved when one has money of his own. These elementary ideas are often startlingly new to young people of the slums. Mrs. Baxter has found that, while many understand the idea of "a job"—something hard to get—few have any real notion that jobs separate into many specialized occupations. They do not know that a house is built from the separate efforts of carpenters, bricklayers, painters, truck drivers, architects, mortgage bankers. No one they know has such a specialized occupation. A low-status, unskilled worker speaks simply of "going to work."

But don't adults of the slums lead their children into wanting something better? Why don't they see school as the obvious avenue of progress? Says Eddie Ponder, the

energetic, zealous director of the Milwaukee experimental
project:

"We can't begin to understand why these people don't
accept school as a real part of their lives until we begin to
understand how they have been rebuffed by every element
of the organized community for more than a hundred
years. They have become convinced, 'You may live here,
but you don't really belong here.' Even the supposedly
helpful, friendly agencies contribute to this negative education. Recently we sent the father of one of our pupils to
a social agency to get advice on budgeting. He had no
conception of how to allot the little money he brought
home. The social agency sent him back with a note saying,
'this family doesn't earn enough to budget. We cannot
give them any advice.' That father, against all the lessons
of his experience, had been willing to give those strange
people in organized society another try, and again they
found him useless as they always had.

"Repeated experiences like that are what helped long
ago to make the people of the slums the lost population.
The schoolchildren grow up absorbing the environment
and experience of their parents. They create a world apart
from agencies, officials, laws, policemen, schools, and
teachers and far away from middle-class ideas of success.
How do you begin to introduce the idea of 'goal' into the
life of a child who grows up in that other world?"

The task of introducing the idea of "goal" must fall, for
lack of anyone else to assume it, upon his teacher. It is a
crushing task, particularly for one untrained for it, who
probably did not choose it, and who frequently does not
comprehend the problem. With the exception of a few
courses of small enrollment in the entire United States,
teachers colleges that are turning out certified educators

by the thousands offer no special instruction in helping the child of the slums. It is no wonder that teachers by the thousands fail. And it is a terrible burden for a weary, bewildered teacher to go home from the classroom after each harassing day carrying the weight of failure. The guilt often turns to hate, and the hate may be turned upon the child.

"My bunch is pretty rough," a husky male teacher in his middle thirties told me in the lunchroom of a Chicago slum school. "But drop in. If you don't mind, I don't mind." Everywhere, I found principals and teachers surprisingly willing to throw open their classrooms. The few good ones want to show the good that can be done. The many helpless ones want to free themselves of the burden of failure; they want to display how terrible the children are.

When I called on the teacher who had invited me, I found him standing in front of his class, hands locked behind him, chest out, shoulders back, springing up and down rhythmically on the balls of his feet, overseeing the sullen, dark-skinned faces that filled the room. It was the authoritative stance of a cop on a beat.

"Most of the time I'm a policeman, not a teacher," he said. "This is what new teachers get to cut their teeth on. Of course, I really don't mind. I was in the army for years and I just got out of teachers college a year ago. Maybe this is a good place for me 'cause I'm a big bruiser. But they'll take some tender young girl right out of college and throw her into a bunch like this to get her started. She has to wait it out until she's got enough seniority to transfer to a decent place. Naturally, the experienced teachers want the better spots. *Someone's* got to do this, so naturally the new ones get it."

All this was said in what I can only call a softened loud tone. The comments were directed at me, but the class heard every word. A dozen times I had heard teachers talk in that special tone. It was more than an expression of contempt; it seemed a form of revenge upon the pupils.

"How do you get them interested when they don't *want* to get interested?" the teacher went on. "Like in art. I put something on the board, some kind of design, and tell them to copy it, except to change it a little so it will be original. They just look at me. They don't understand. They don't try to understand, so what can I do?"

His class of sixth-graders seemed old enough for high school. The boys were big-boned, muscular, some at the age of shaving. The girls were plump and bosomy. They sat in a hodge-podge of slovenly postures, facing almost every way except straight forward, where the teacher's desk was. Yet there was a liveliness in the room. An unspoken language of defiance seemed to flit through the air, by subtle flicking of eyes, the dropping of a book, two heads disappearing in the depths of the aisle, an elaborate yawn and stretching of arms, half-concealed smirks spreading across the room. The teacher seemed as blind to this language as the children seemed deaf to his.

"I try to emphasize reading—reading is what keeps them three or four years behind in grade—but they have no attention span." Then for the first time he lowered his voice, half turning his back to the class, preparing to say something unspeakable. "What do you think the average I Q is in a group like this?" he whispered. "About 75. I mean that's the *average*, so you can imagine how low they get. You know, 75 is the borderline of mentally retarded. Yes, I know the I Q doesn't show everything. But it's a pretty fair indication of what you can *expect*."

On the teacher's desk lay a shaft of two-by-four lumber whittled to a jagged shape. "Some kid brought this to protect himself with," said the teacher, pounding the weapon into his palm, his voice full again. "Naturally, I took it away from him, but now I keep it handy to protect myself. A teacher got bopped again in the rest room this morning. You never know what to *expect*."

Teachers everywhere I went seemed preoccupied with the idea of "what to expect," so seldom with what they might effect. And as Mrs. Stangel in Milwaukee had said pointedly, "A child does what's expected of him." Recently a psychologist at the University of North Dakota, Dr. Robert Rosenthal, showed vividly how an expectation becomes a reality. He selected two groups of psychology students and put each in charge of teaching a group of rats to run through a maze. Dr. Rosenthal then told one group its rats were "maze-bright," the other that its rats were "maze-dull." Both these statements were unfounded, but Dr. Rosenthal wanted to give each group of students something "to expect." Sure enough, the students who thought they had "maze-bright" rats got significantly better results than those misled into expecting their rats were dull.

And the schoolteacher's index of what to expect from pupils, of course, is the I Q. Recently, however, Ernest A. Haggard, a psychologist, found he could raise I Qs substantially in slum schools by giving children a mere three hours of coaching and practice in how to take the I Q test, by offering small rewards for doing well, and by training examiners to convey simple friendliness to the children. While teachers often explain away a child's poor reading by showing his low I Q, Dr. Haggard turned this proposition around. He raised I Qs even further by having examiners read test items aloud while children followed them in their test booklets. Their I Qs had been depressed *because* they were poor readers.

To convey her contempt for children she has failed to

teach, a teacher does not have to be openly hostile. She can do it with condescension and even better with pity. These were the stock in trade of one Chicago principal of an all-white slum school. I had heard about her all over the Midwest as a model of "understanding" and "feeling." She attends educational conferences in the Southern Appalachians, visits the mountain hovels many of her pupils emigrated from, and quickly serves notice on visitors that "you mustn't use the word 'hillbillies' in regard to my children, because I can't afford to have my name associated with that word."

She began my tour of her school by pointing out "one of our sweet little Indian girls." Before a class of fidgeting youngsters, she drew an attractive child to her side. "Isn't she a darling?" she asked. "We're especially pleased with how clean she is—haven't you noticed?" Turning to the girl, she inquired sweetly, "But you aren't a full-blooded Indian, are you, dear?"

Leading me into the library, she announced, "These are our special problem boys, but we do believe in them. Yes, with some the problem may be reading or it may be other things. Everyone's here to get some little thing doctored. Isn't that right, boys?" The boys, young teenagers, remained expressionless.

"I wonder if you've noticed," she went on, "what nice haircuts everyone here has. We don't let their being poor stand in the way of their looking presentable. If one of them can't afford the few pennies for a haircut, we have barbers in the neighborhood who cut their hair free. We try to teach our boys pride and self-respect. Everyone is ready to help them."

The school had a feeling, not of a place for educational growth, but of a prison with a benign lady warden. Even schoolwork is used as a protective weapon by teachers

against "bad" children. "In social studies," a bright thir-
teen-year-old girl in seventh grade told me, "we get a
chapter a week to read for homework, but nothing to
write. Unless we're noisy. Then we get written work for
punishment. Twice I had to do a five-hundred word essay
on why I talk so much. If the teacher catches us talking
when she's out of the room we get themes to write. We get
themes at other times too, just because she's in a bad
mood."

Mrs. Bailey Bishop, teacher of the first grade at Coleman
School, an antiquated building in the heart of Chicago's
Negro ghetto, looks like neither a continual violator of
convention nor like one of the most startlingly successful
teachers in the world. She is both.

If her class were "experimental," supported by a foundation, her methods would be the subject of lengthy papers.
But hers is an ordinary class of ordinary slum kids, dealt to
her at random. Their I Q scores are low. Their "cultural
deprivation" is high. Their families are paralyzed by poverty.

The day I visited Mrs. Bishop's first-graders, they were
reading aloud about space capsules and oxygen. The word
"weightlessness" was hardly any trouble to them at all.
Why not? Mrs. Bishop had first made them curious about
gravity, weight, and finally weightlessness. Once they
grasped the idea, the children had need for a word to
describe it. She gave them the word. They treasure its
sound, its sight, and its correct spelling.

Mrs. Bishop not only ignores I Qs, but she believes there
is no such thing as a first-grade vocabulary. She believes
children will learn words they need to know, and their
needs depend on the excitement in their minds. To excite
their minds, Mrs. Bishop almost never teaches. She asks

questions—carefully choosing questions the children can answer. She leads them in constructing old information into new ideas; they experience the joys of "finding out," enjoy the feeling of success with every question and every answer.

Since Mrs. Bishop ignores the prescribed first-grade vocabulary, she ignores first-grade textbooks. The room is strewn with books of many levels. During breaks in activity, children go to a "reading table" and choose a book that interests them. If the ideas are interesting, they *learn* the words. (They seldom choose books that say "Look, Dick, Look—Run, Jane, Run.")

Mrs. Bishop began her class by chalking on the blackboard:

I am going to talk to you on the board this morning.

As she wrote, the children read each word aloud, often anticipating the word before she had finished writing it. Their heads strained forward. These were not silly words in a book about strange people. Mrs. Bishop was talking to *them;* if they could make out the words, they'd know what she was trying to say. This was a fascinating game. She wrote:

Things we have to do today.

Hands leaped up. What followed was an exercise in eagerness, planning, organization of time and duty, reading and enunciation of lots of big words that never appeared in a first-grade reader. As Mrs. Bishop recognized each hand raised, the child suggested a duty for the day. Mrs. Bishop listed the duty on the board, the children pronouncing each word without difficulty because it had a meaning for them:

We will do our work papers.
We have to read the bulletin boards.
We must read the chart stories.

We have to fix the thermometer.

We have to take care of the pets.

We have to paint a picture for the mural.

Before one fascinating activity had quite finished, Mrs. Bishop had another under way. Introducing the "new mathematics" to the first grade, Mrs. Bishop drew a strange diagram on the board:

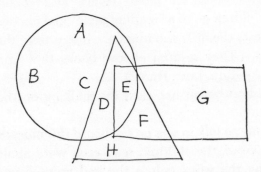

"I am thinking of a letter," she said. "Can you think of three good questions to ask me so you'll know which letter I'm thinking of?"

An explosion of hands. "Is it inside the circle?" . . . "Is it inside the triangle?" . . . "Is it inside the rectangle?" To each of these Mrs. Bishop answered, with rising suspense, "Yes."

One child, hardly able to contain the force of his suspicion, asked, "Is it inside *everything?*"

Mrs. Bishop, eyes agleam, luring him on, nodded yes.

The child triumphantly shouted, "It's *E!*"

She played the game three times. The children, captivated by the pleasures of abstract logic, asked please to play it still another time, then once more again. Finally, putting down her chalk, Mrs. Bishop said quietly, "See? If you ask good questions, you can find things out."

The unrelenting excitement in the room, the brightness

of the minds, the visible growth of the children's experience, made it easy for one to forget that these were "culturally deprived" children in one of the worst of slum districts. They seemed a class of the especially gifted—which of course they were. They were gifted with a teacher who really liked them, who believed that all children *including* slum children *want* to learn whatever appears exciting and useful, and who came to them in the first grade to help mold them, instead of in a seventh-grade remedial-reading class when it was too late.

Dr. Martin Deutsch suspects that even the first grade may be too late for a child's introduction to the ideas, habits, and objects of a wordy world. Dr. Deutsch's Institute of Developmental Studies is running four experimental nursery classes for four- and five-year-olds in Harlem school buildings. Carefully trained teachers enliven their children's minds as Mrs. Bishop instinctively does with her Chicago first-graders.

A similar experiment is in progress in Baltimore. Both experiments are subsidized by the Ford Foundation, which is also underwriting the special classes in Milwaukee and numerous other large, slum-ridden cities. The most publicized of these experimental projects has been Higher Horizons, a large dose of "cultural enrichment" given to junior-high-school students in New York City slum areas. In Junior High School No. 43, where the project began in 1956, more than half the students raised their I Qs, some an astonishing 40 points. Grades rose impressively, discipline problems diminished, the students did far better in high school than preproject students, and the number who went on to college multiplied by three and a half times.

New York's Board of Education, confident it had found the formula for educating slum children, rapidly introduced Higher Horizons to sixty-three schools. Too rapidly. Money for extra remedial-reading teachers and guidance counselors on so large a scale could not be found. Principals and classroom teachers had not been sufficiently trained out of their old habits and ideas. There was some evidence, too, that the sudden exposure to large doses of classical music, art galleries, and literature assignments at the junior-high-school level was too much, too late. After the expansion, the Higher Horizons spectacular record of results was considerably watered down.

In St. Louis an ex-basketball coach appears to have come closer than anyone else to a large-scale, enduring success. Samuel Shepard, Jr., superintendent of twenty-three virtually all-Negro elementary schools, has lifted school attendance of his children from the lowest in the city to the city's average. Their academic abilities rose steadily until June 1961 when eighth-grade graduates tested at the national norms for reading and arithmetic, and slightly higher than national norms for language skills. This has been accomplished with no significant change in classroom materials or study plans.

Shepard dispatched staff members to teacher after teacher, showing charts of fourth-grade readers reading at second-grade level, seventh-graders at fourth-grade level.

"You used to say," Shepard told teachers' meetings, "that you couldn't teach unless your classes were reduced from 45 to 35. We now have a city-wide average of 35. In this district, because of our special problems, we've won a reduction to 33. If you can't teach better to classes that size, maybe the problem is that you can't teach."

The former basketball coach followed up this challenging locker-room pep talk by requiring teachers to spend afterschool time visiting homes of their pupils. Ostensibly these visits were to advise parents on how to help their children do homework by allotting time and

study space. Really, Shepard wanted his teachers exposed
—many for the first time—to the seemingly hopeless home
and neighborhood lives of their pupils. He wanted to rid
teachers of the middle-class cliché, "A teacher can't
substitute for the good, wholesome influence of parents."
Teachers *must* provide the substitute influence, if the new
generation is not to be surrendered to old cultural patterns
drilled into Negro Americans since slavery—passive-
ness, dependence, absence of career ambition (made
praiseworthy by the white man's phrase, "He knows how
to keep his place").

"If the white world could understand," Shepard said,
"how the nonwhite has had hostility trampled into him for
a hundred years, then the white world would begin to
understand the problem they have given us to unravel in
the lives of these children. Maybe they'd understand how
hard it is to convince a kid, in the face of all his home and
community influences, that he really belongs in the same
world a white man belongs in."

To help tear the children away from the negative
influences of home and neighborhood, Shepard enlisted
the homes and neighborhoods themselves. Teachers, during visits to homes, urged parents to come to school meetings to learn how to help their children by encouraging
study. Parents were taken aback; they had never beeen
asked to school before unless a child was in trouble. Shepard arranged study places in libraries and community
buildings, then urged parents of crowded homes to bring
children there. He distributed homework assignment
booklets to children; parents were to sign them each week
affirming that they had inspected the child's homework.
Shepard was less concerned with the inspection than with
making the parent feel he was participating and needed.

Shepard wrote letters to parents by the hundreds. "I'd

find any excuse to write to them," he says, "anything that would describe a success. These people had never had the simple experience of being told that someone in their family had achieved something. We set up honor rolls for anything we could honor the children for, so that every kid was either on a list or knew someone who was. And I don't mean the suburban kid he knew of whose house gets cleaned by one of our kid's mothers. I mean here.

"We set up an honor roll for high grades, others for perfect attendance, for art work, for compositions, and one for most improvement—that's usually a list of former hell raisers who nobody thought could ever be straightened out."

As the academic achievement began to rise, a strange thing happened. Teachers with seniority stopped asking to transfer to "nicer" neighborhoods, as teachers do in almost all slum districts. Instead Shepard found himself bombarded by applications for transfers into his district at more than five times the rate of vacancies. Just as the pupils and parents hungered for the nourishment of success, so did teachers.

Shepard's big gun is a campaign to convince parents and pupils that a profound change has taken place in the job picture for Negroes. Fifteen years ago a Negro struggling to earn an engineering degree might be wasting his time; discrimination would bar him from professional jobs. Today, when the demand for skills is great, jobs are opening up for people of any color—if they are skilled. But the deadly weight of past frustrations has kept Negroes from training for them.

Shepard and his staff organized a "road show" of seventeen young Negroes, each solidly trained, each in a skilled job, but not so advanced that a twelve-year-old slum child could not imagine doing the same. The "road show" traveled from school to school appearing before parents and pupils. One of Shepard's young principals, Ernest Jones, vividly describes the meetings:

"We tell the parents, 'Now we've been saying that if your child works hard in school it will pay off in the long run. We're going to try to show you.' The audience is skeptical. Whatever you say, they'll shake their heads for an hour and say 'Yessir, that's right,' the way they've learned to do when white people talk to them, but you're not communicating. Then we bring in each of these seventeen people, start interviewing them before the crowd, and a change takes place.

" 'Where do you work?'

" 'McDonnell Aircraft.'

" 'What do they do?'

" 'They make space capsules.'

"The young fellow illustrates on a blackboard what space capsules are and how he helps design them. We ask if he needs any training for such work. He tells about the schooling he had. Then we ask: 'Did you get that kind of job the first time you went somewhere to apply for one?' You can hear the hall freeze with attention. He says, 'No. But I knew I was properly trained and qualified. I knew there was a place for me somewhere and I found it at McDonnell.'

"Most of the adults in that hall have never heard a young Negro from their own neighborhood say anything like that before—because for the most part it was never true before. Next we bring on a computer programer who not only has a good job but recently won an award as the outstanding government employee in the St. Louis area.

"The one who really shakes the people up is a woman who's an artist for Pet Milk Company. We ask her, 'How many children were in your family?' She says 'Nine.' You feel a slight tremble in the hall from an excuse caving in. Then she adds she was the oldest and had to look after all the others. Another excuse hits the ground. She says, 'I remember I had two dresses. While I wore one, I washed and dried the other one for school next day.' You can't imagine the impact on the people when she tells that. That's the story of every woman in the hall."

"Our slogan," adds Samuel Shepard, "is 'No excuses.' It's not an easy slogan to put over after a hundred years of frustration. But we have to face the fact squarely that discrimination is not only a hindrance to getting a job but can also be used as an excuse for not expecting to get one. We want to convince people to throw away all the crutches. We want to show that successful people have come from all kinds of undesirable conditions, but they made it anyhow."

"The greatest joy that you can have in this kind of work," young Ernest Jones concludes, "is seeing a kid get out of high school, his whole world changed from when he went in. I keep thinking of a boy I saw one night at a roller-skating party. He was about seventeen. I hadn't seen him since he got out of my grammar school four years earlier. He was headed, frankly, toward being a bum. No interest, no motivation, no real concern about anything, always out in the street. It's tough when you know a kid's got it but he's not using it. At this skating party I asked the boy how he'd been doing and he said 'Fine,' that he was about to graduate from high school. I was surprised he'd stayed in school and I said so. 'Mr. Jones,' he said—he was very polite and lively—'I'm going to keep going to school for a while. I figure if I don't do that I'm going to wind up just not doing much.' My God—it really got through to him. We work day and night to get through to these kids. Yet it's always a surprise when we run into a kid saying something like that. The job sometimes is so hard that maybe even we don't believe it's possible to get through. Then one kid comes along and tells you all those days and nights have a purpose after all."

6

"where can we go?
what can we do?"

The great triumph of our educational
system reached its climax between a half century and a
quarter century ago. The cities of America, particularly in
the Northeast, were vast Babels of immigrants. In a
generation, our educational system—schools as well as less
tangible institutions—taught them a common language,
common aspirations, complementary trades, workably
harmonious ways. It performed upon these immigrants
and their children the mysterious process that we call
"Americanizing," and they repaid their new country by
further enriching it.

When the wave of immigration subsided, a new tidal
wave had begun, the mammoth flow of native Americans
from farm to city. It is still rolling in full force. In 1935 there

were 6.8 million plots of land that the Census Bureau
called farms. Now there are fewer than 3.7 million. Experts
guess that by 1980 there may be fewer than a million. One
American on a farm used to feed three others in town.
Today one farmer feeds 27 and will soon feed 50.

Oddly, our educational system, which was so successful
in Americanizing foreigners, is failing to urbanize vast
numbers of country-bred Americans. Inquire into the
background of a dislocated, unemployed illiterate in the
city. The chances are he was born on a submarginal farm;
if not, his parents had left a submarginal farm, come to the
city, and were segregated among other ex-submarginal
farmers behind such impregnable ghetto walls that "Amer-
icanization" could not break through.

Therefore, those alarmed about city unemployment
"caused" by automation must concern themselves with a
brambled, thorny problem they are often inclined to push
out of sight: the so-called farm problem. That is where the
city problem starts.

A congressman from Kansas, J. Floyd Breeding, recently
said: "Fuss about the disappearing farm or any other
phase of the problem you wish, but what it all adds up to is
technological unemployment in agriculture. It requires
only a few of us to produce food and fiber for all the rest of
us. Those who might otherwise be employed in agriculture
now must find other places than the farm to live, other jobs
than farming to do. The result has been a vast, un-
precedented social and economic upheaval, the effects
of which no one has yet begun to measure."

The upheaval was soon to hit Breeding himself in a way
he had not yet begun to measure. So many families were
leaving farms in Kansas that the state recently lost one of
its six Congressional seats. Breeding's district was the one
eliminated. Thus he became a technologically unemployed

ex-congressman. (But like most Kansas ex-farmers, who are seldom lacking in basic education, Mr. Breeding had little trouble finding work.)

In trying to find out what the farm problem really is, we may begin with what most of us think it is. Let's begin by meeting a young man who is to the farm problem what Don Jones was to the factory problem: a man in temporary trouble who is mistakenly publicized as the victim of the technological upheaval, when his life has really been improved by it. His trouble, nevertheless, is real, as a talk with him makes clear.

"I have the feeling I'm being pushed around by some-body bigger than me, but I don't know who he is." As the young farmer, puzzled and tense, spoke to me, across the room his dark-haired, dark-eyed wife, listening, watching, seemed to be gauging the depth of her husband's strain. Their four young children eyed us curiously.

"Sometimes," he continued, "I feel like I live in one of those Western towns you see in the movies where a man with a big gun struts around and says, 'I run this place. My name is Tex spelled with a capital T, and you all do what I say.' Trouble is, if you ask me who's Tex, I don't know."

The man, thirty-five-year-old Ervin Stadelman of South Wayne, Wisconsin, tall and lean, unusually fair except for childlike bursts of rosiness in his cheeks, is the kind of farmer widely regarded as a national symbol of inde-pendence. He has no boss to order him about, no cus-tomers to sweet-talk. He runs what is known as a family farm. He and his wife Jeanne milk cows for a living. He feeds his cows corn, oats, and hay that he cultivates himself on 225 acres he rents from his father. Every day a tank truck from the city drives up to his milkhouse and takes every drop, no dickering, no questions asked. Every month, the postman brings a check from the milk company in Chicago.

"These farm magazines keep telling me how independent I am. The family farm, they say, is the backbone of America. If the family farm goes down, everything goes down. Yet what am I? I try to be a professional, but to my milk company I'm a statistic. I'm Patron Number 327. When the truck comes to take my milk, I don't even know how much I'm selling it for. A month later I find out. It says on the check how much my milk was worth. I can't tell the milk company I want a little more money. They're told the price every month by the Federal Milk Marketing Order. But the government doesn't set the price either. They just do the arithmetic according to some formula that hardly anybody understands. I could make more profit if I lowered my costs, if I invested in bigger, better machines. But the credit companies say I have to pay off a new machine in three years, even if the machine will last fifteen. Those big payments kill a small farmer. I don't know who's to blame. I just know if you put them all together—the milk companies, the Department of Agriculture, the marketing orders, the credit companies, even the retired farmers who run the big farm organizations that never seem to get us anywhere—they're all Tex. They tell me what to do, how much I collect, who to pay, how fast to pay it. They all have more to say about running my farm than I do."

Stadelman collected about $14,000 last year for his milk. According to the economics of a family farm, that figure should put him on high ground. But Jeanne told me, "When the milk check comes each month and we finish making the credit payments, I'm lucky if I have a hundred dollars for groceries and things for the house."

Erv and Jeanne Stadelman's personal finances should

properly remain their private affair but have become, in a sense, everybody's business. The government is spending more than $6 billion a year—$125 in taxes for every American family—in the name of protecting the independence of the family farmer. Yet, in every state, barns and homes stand empty and abandoned, their cultivated rows of earth blended with those of bigger farmers getting still bigger. In the city, the slums, employment offices, charity centers, bars, the free wards of hospitals, all are alive with the musically turned syllables of country talk.

The story of Erv and Jeanne Stadelman, even though they surely do not resemble the chronically unemployed, can help us understand the sweep of population from farm to city. Erv and Jeanne met eleven years ago at the University of Wisconsin, got married, and left school to take over the farm where Erv had grown up. As his Swiss-born father had done, Erv concentrated on raising hogs, which were bringing 25 cents a pound, a good price. He had hardly started, however, when the price began to slip. Before long hogs were bringing only 18 cents. Jeanne remembers the day Erv herded ten tons of squawling porkers to market. That night she figured the cost of renting the land, paying a hired man, feeding the animals, compared the costs against the check Erv had brought home, and was dismayed to discover they had fattened all those fine porkers for nothing. They had ended up empty-handed.

That was right after the Korean conflict. Countries ravaged during World War II had returned to tilling their lands. The farm radio programs, the farm papers, were all spreading a strange new word: surplus. American farmers were doing too well at their task. They were producing too much food, more than Americans were eating or exporting. Prices were caving in. The only way a farmer could protect himself was to cut his costs—make his farm more efficient, make his land produce still *more*. In a desperate attempt to climb out of an airless pit of abundance, the farmer seemed to have no choice but to dig deeper into it.

For the past fifteen years America's farmers have felt like the sorcerer's apprentice who had learned how to command a magic broomstick to carry in water, but didn't know how to tell it to stop. In 1948 the federal government began buying up wheat, rice, cotton, tobacco, and dairy products just to get them out of the market place, trying to protect a "fair" price for farmers. In a year a billion dollars in taxes were spent for food and fibers that nobody in the market was ready to buy.

To slow down production, the government began "renting" millions of acres of farm land—paying farmers a fee for not planting them. But the magic broomstick wouldn't stop carrying water. Farmers poured bigger quantities of better fertilizers into less land, and the food flowered in ever-increasing abundance.

Did a billion dollars seem like a lot of surplus in 1948? By 1962, farmers were piling up five times that surplus on less land. Taxpayers were now putting out a billion dollars a year just to *store* the accumulated food that wouldn't stop coming and that nobody would buy.

When Erv and Jeanne Stadelman realized that they were going broke raising porkers, Erv decided to get rid of them and turn to building a herd of cows. For one thing, the work was pleasanter. But, more important that that, the government was buying surpluses of dairy products, so milk prices were steadier.

By acquiring a herd of cows, Stadelman seemed to aggravate the dairy surplus problem. Really, of course, the government had aggravated it by rewarding him, in the form of protected prices, for adding to the surplus. The overabundance grew even worse when Erv, a conscientious man, determined to be the most efficient dairyman he could. By careful breeding, he raised his annual output from 7,000 pounds of milk per cow to 11,000 pounds. His herd grew from a few to forty fine animals.

Erv and Jeanne aimed not only at "efficiency" but at making life a little easier. They felt both were equally important to survival.

"I don't want Jeanne to be my hired man," Erv says with suppressed anger. "Go into a hospital and see how many farmers' wives have miscarriages and back troubles. Look at their arms. They're as muscular and tough and hairy as their husbands'. They get that way from carrying cans of milk, baling the hay, all the things a hired man does. She's a pretty girl and I want her to stay the way she is."

Erv had no plans to ruin himelf either. All his life he had seen farmers with small tractors trundle across their fields all day, then turn on headlights and labor through the night. That was the mark of a "good" farmer.

"I know one 'good' farmer near here," Erv told me, "who goes to a chiropractor twice a week for back trouble. His father died at an early age and this fellow says he'll be proud to leave this world the same way, working hard. Almost any night you can see him out there, headlights on, riding his little old-fashioned tractor, plowing. If those are the things a 'good' farmer has to do, maybe I want to be a bad farmer."

To the shock of his father and tradition-bound neighbors, Erv invested 5,000 borrowed dollars in a modern tractor. When Jeanne was in her third pregnancy, Erv borrowed more to build a brick milking parlor. Through glasslike pipelines, it pumped milk from automatic milking devices to a great stainless steel tub, called a bulk cooler. No more lifting of milk cans. The sanitary cooler, which Jeanne scrubs down twice each day, qualified the Stadelmans for a Grade A milk certificate, which meant a higher price. Payments for the improvements were a severe burden, but they could see better days perhaps three years ahead.

Then last summer came a disastrous drought. Corn grew in short, scrawny stalks; the hay and oat harvest was thin.

"Some farmers," Jeanne told me, "fed their cattle less and watched the animals get bony. But Erv couldn't bring himself to do that. He wants his cows sleek, sassy, and fat. If we went out and bought someone else's corn for cash, there'd be no profit in our milk. That's how close our costs are figured. There was only one thing Erv could do. After working for years to build up his herd to forty good cows, he sold off fifteen of them, so the rest would have enough to eat. We don't know how many years it will take us to recover from that blow."

That economic loss was directly tied to the education of their children—as we will soon find the national farm problem is tied to the education of all farm children.

The Stadelmans had been paying a tuition fee to send their two school-age children to a public school of another county. Now that luxury—which Jeanne had regarded as a necessity—had to go. The local school she had to put them in—and which she had tried to avoid—was a one-room school. Fourteen pupils, first- to eighth-graders, meet together and compete for the attention of a single teacher. There are hundreds of schools like this in Wisconsin, thousands throughout the farm regions of America. The teacher is required to have completed merely two years in a county-run teachers college. She is responsible to a school board of three who usually have not been educated beyond twelfth grade.

I asked Erv Stadelman a question I had asked farmers

across the country: With all these frustrations, why stay on the farm? Why not quit, do something with less headache and heartache? His reply was what I had expected to hear from everyone, but heard hardly at all:

"I like to see things start fresh," he told me after a moment of searching thought. "When I walk around the farm I like to think of what's under the ground more than what's above it, of what can be done, all the things that haven't begun to grow yet. Something that hits me is walking across a pasture and seeing a little heifer about to be born. Its face is starting to poke out of its mother. You give it a little pull, help it along, and wipe its nose off. It's a new beginning, a starting all over again."

He paused, and turned his thoughts in a new direction.

"You know, I love football. I'm crazy about the Green Bay Packers because they play like champions. I admire any kind of champions. They fight to win and hate to lose. I see running this farm as a fight to keep from losing. But I'm not too worried about losing for the reasons you think. If I lose, it won't be because I couldn't hang on, but because I got fed up. I might just get tired of trying to be as good a dairyman as I can against all these odds. If I get tired, if I lose my dream, then I'm done."

He was staying on the farm not because he had to, but because he really wanted to.

The great myth about the American farmer that we enjoy perpetuating, no matter how much it costs, is the myth that he is still an independent man. Almost everybody keeps saying it, including the farmer, and almost everybody seems to believe it, except the farmer.

In Akron, Colorado, a wheat farmer's son and daughter, both working their way through college, told me about the severity of last year's drought and how a hailstorm the year before had all but destroyed their father's crop. They didn't know how long he could hang on to his 160 acres. Did the boy plan to take over the farm some day? No, he was going into law. Then why did the father struggle so hard to hold his land? Wouldn't he be better off somewhere else? The girl looked at me puzzled, almost frightened. "But where will he go?" she asked. "If he leaves the farm, what else can he do?"

That was the answer I heard almost everywhere when I asked "Why stay on the farm?" I heard it from farmers, heads of their organizations, government officeholders: "If a farmer is forced off the land, where will he go, what will he do?"

Those are not words of independence. They describe families who are trapped.

The good farmer today like Erv Stadelman, is a man of some education. In the age of technology a man of reasonable education can make out almost anywhere. The farmers in deepest trouble are those prepared only to water their rows of earth by the sweat of their brows, cultivate with muscle instead of machine. They are the ones who are trapped. Not trapped by the land, nor by surpluses, nor low prices, even though all these are causing severe stress. Like unemployed coal miners, they are trapped by their lack of education. They are untrained to work anywhere but on old-fashioned farms that the country no longer needs.

"But if the government stops propping up their prices," a Wisconsin agricultural agent asked me, "are the cities ready to absorb all these people who never held city jobs? Are all these people to go on relief?"

That question, posed constantly by farm authorities, vibrates with ironies. When it's asked, one pictures a vast prairie of once-proud farmers, each riding a tractor, each sadly surveying his 160, or 200, or 240 acres of wheat or corn, each worth tens of thousands of dollars in investment, each a pillar of family independence, but now being taken away like a prisoner. The image plucks the heartstrings of rural congressmen, coffers crack open and billions pour out. So the farmers *do* go on relief without ever leaving the farm. Everybody gets some of the money, the well-set middle-class farmer, the not-so-well-set "marginal" farmer, and even lots of millionaire farmers. Everybody gets something except the farmer who inspires the outpouring, the poverty-stricken man who is really behind most of the statistics.

Here we encounter a strange case of popular confusion which must be straightened out if we are to see the problem of farmers as it really is. Whenever most of us hear that every year hundreds of thousands of small, "independent" farmers are being driven from the farm, we conjure an image of a family like Erv Stadelman's. But severe as Stadelman's struggle is, he is not the man being run into town. Nor is he even a "small" farmer, as farmers go. Farms like Stadelman's, run by educated, scientific men, selling products valued at more than $10,000 a year, comprise the cream of family farms, the top 20 per cent. It is the only group of farms that is *growing* in number. From 1949 to 1959 their number almost doubled, leaping from 334,000 to 648,000.

But if the familiar faces of Erv and Jeanne Stadelman—typical farm folks who are not really so typical—are not the ones behind the alarming statistics, then whose are? Who are the farm families herding into strange cities to suffer the oblivion of chronic unemployment?

Of the millions recently driven from the land, the overwhelming number crowding our cities to suffer the agonizing oblivion of unemployment resemble the people we

found on relief in Chicago, trying to learn their A B Cs—
the parents of benighted children in city slum schools.
They are long-impoverished mountaineers from the rocky,
unyielding soil of the Southern Appalachians and the
Ozarks, defenders of a nineteenth-century culture for
whom an improbable life has recently turned to impossible. And, far more numerously, they are penniless, un-
lettered Negroes from the Deep South, ousted by new
machines from the only work they, their parents, or their
slave grandparents were ever taught to do, picking cotton
by hand.

No congressman rises to bewail the loss of their "independence." They have no big farm organization to lobby
for them. They count for nothing except in statistics, and
even there they are mistaken for someone else. As soon as
their vast numbers are misused to scare up money for
helping others, they are swept under the national rug,
forgotten until they turn up in the city with no choice but
to go on relief. Until then, nobody pries into their personal
finances, as reporters constantly do with middle-class
farmers, for who cares about a farmer so small that he's not
big enough in the government's eyes even to qualify as a
small farmer?

A short time ago, I visited a Mississippi sharecropper,
counted by the Census as a family farmer—therefore not
listed among the unemployed—a thin, elderly Negro with
balding head and patient, benign eyes. By the hundreds of
thousands his relatives, friends, and neighbors are invading Chicago, St. Louis, Memphis, Detroit, New York,
Washington—where, without worsening their condition,
they change from farm statistics to unemployment
statistics—but he is too old to think of going.

"The landowner he gives me twelve, fifteen acres to
farm," the sharecropper told me, describing the system

that is driving his neighbors away. "That's all the cotton two people, me and my wife, can handle by hand. We had five children, but one by one they all died. We're allowed to take a little corner of the land and grow some vegetables for ourselves, feed a few chickens, to get through the winter. It used to be we could raise hogs to eat but the man won't let us do that any more. He wants the land for cotton.

"After we pick the cotton the man takes it to town and later tells us how much he allows us out of the price he got. He might say he got thirty-five cents a pound and allow us twenty cents. We plant it, grow it, watch it, chop it, bale it, and then he tells us how much he'll allow us. We might say to him, 'I heard on the radio that cotton was getting fifty cents today.' He says, 'Maybe you heard that but your cotton wasn't up to grade.' Sometimes he says, 'Sure, but I got to pay for my time riding around here taking care of things.' Everybody around here knows the big plantations got new machines to plant and pick cotton. There's hardly no people working on those places any more. If we give the man too much trouble, he can just put in one of those machines. So we got to come cheaper than the machine do if we want to stay, I guess.

"No, we got no piece of paper that we sign with him. In our kind of sharecropping nobody has a piece of paper. It's whatever the man says, that's what we got to do. But we do better than some people. My wife and I come out with five or seven hundred dollars a year. Lots of people only take out two, three, four hundred. The man knows we don't get enough to live on, so in the winter he lends us some. That way he keeps us from ever leaving. We can't leave if we owe him money."

About 350,000 families—more than a million people— are still farming for earnings that average less than nine

dollars a week, and earning an average of only ten dollars a
week in extra jobs off the farm. Those are earnings for the
entire family. What keeps them on the farm is not a myth
of independence, nor a desire to pass on a legacy of the
land to their children, nor any myth at all. They are lashed
to the land by the realities of ignorance. They have no
other place to go, nothing else they know how to do.

At a meeting of representatives of such indigent farmers
gathered from all over the South, I heard an unimaginative
Department of Agriculture official begin a talk with a stock
attention-getter. "The United States," he said, "is the only
major power in the world that is beset with the problem of
too much food instead of too little."

The sharecroppers nodded respectfully, moaning for
emphasis, "Mmmm *mmmh.*" "Uh-*hunh,*" as they might in
the presence of a preacher uttering a profound though obvious truth. But after his speech the people took up a
more pressing matter. They wanted to know how their
towns, their counties, their states, anybody, could get hold
of some of these surplus foods—cereals, beans, eggs, powdered milk. Children on their neighboring farms were literally going hungry. The federal government was willing
to give the food to the needy, but the law requires that a
local government transport and distribute it. Many Southern communities, enthusiasts of the principle of such local
initiative, have not taken the trouble. Since the outbreak
of civil-rights demonstrations, conditions have worsened.
Many local governments have clearly implied to Negroes
that old-fashioned docility is the price of packages of surplus food.

In Mississippi County, Arkansas, a rich cotton territory,
new harvesting machines have brought such poverty that
27,000 people—40 per cent of the county's population—
are eligible to receive federal surplus food. Playing

machine against man, plantation owners and local officials have driven wages as low as 30 cents an hour. Surplus food has been a handy tool in keeping wages low. The district's congressman, E. C. Gathings, a member of the House Agriculture Committee, appreciatively related how local officials removed 17,000 from the food lists "and said to them, 'Until such time as you get out there to help us harvest our crops you cannot receive these foods.'" Similarly in nearby St. Francis County, 14,000 were dropped from food rolls and the Arkansas *Gazette* headlined, COUNTY JUDGE SLASHES SURPLUS FOOD LIST TO PROVIDE LOCAL LABOR FOR COTTON HARVEST.

Thus one surplus—food—is used as a club for forcing people to harvest another surplus—cotton. Farm workers are cheated, yet the government buys, the consumer in town and country is taxed twice—in real taxes, and artificially supported prices; the cotton-growing "family farmer" profits so nicely he plants another crop of surplus, the broomstick keeps carrying in buckets and buckets of water, and the sorceror's apprentice just stands there, speechless and helpless.

This discussion will not propose how to stop the surpluses. Everyone knows how to end the surpluses, yet no one knows. Obviously the bins would soon empty if we could feed the hungry people of the world, propagate livestock in the far corners of all the continents and use the surplus grains to fatten them. Yet as soon as we propose sending the food away—by sale or gift—a faraway states-man cries out that we will destroy the frail farm economy of this country or that. So the bins stay full and the storage costs spill over.

But the subject here is not surpluses or prices or acreage

or production efficiency. The subject is farm families. People. Individuals. What are they to do?

Jeanne Stadelman instinctively struck at the heart of the matter when she squeezed her family budget as long as she could, paying tuition to send her children to another county's public school so they could avoid the one-room school nearby. She properly saw that a child once crippled educationally becomes enslaved by the land, by the hopeless economics of obsolete farms.

Too many farm experts try to save the farmer's child by manipulating commodities and dollars. Almost none seek the child's salvation in cultivating a new, better, more enriched crop of people. The experts juggle prices, shuffle acreage, load corn cribs to overflowing, and ask compassionately, "If we don't keep these poor people on the farm, what else can they do?" But they present few ideas for equipping people, through education, to make a choice of doing something else.

At the cost of merely *storing* the present surpluses for a single year—a billion dollars—surely every one-room school in the country could be replaced by modern consolidated schools. With such a sum, the salary of every country schoolteacher could be raised sufficiently to attract some of the best prepared, instead of the least.

The real farm problem is not the surplus of goods but a surplus of people. The statistics that should alarm us most are not of highly capitalized farmers harvesting too much food, but of empty-pocket farmers who for years have had too little to eat. And where we find the poorest farmers, we find the poorest schools.

Near the Ozarks, a center of empty-pocket poor farmers and poorest of poor schools, I visited James Doarn, regional director of the Department of Health, Education, and Welfare. "Instead of working so hard to keep 'em down on the farm," he said, "maybe we ought to accept the inevitable, shift our emphasis to giving kids a fair chance to compete under new conditions in new places. When kids from poor farm communities arrive in the cities with lower educational and economic standards, they're stuck. They're unable to compete for jobs. They're socially out of place in a strange world. What's there to save them from being first on the unemployment rolls, first on the aid-to-dependent-children rolls, first in jail, and maybe first in the mental hospitals?"

The Ozarks are educationally ahead of some areas of the South that do not even have laws making school attendance compulsory. Yet in one pair of Missouri Ozark counties, of 80 grammar schools, 70 are one-room schools. One Ozark school was spending $291 a year to educate each child, another $269, still another $242. In contrast, about $700 is spent on a child in the suburbs of St. Louis, only 100 miles away.

Some defend one-room schools with the same magical word that hallows the family farmer: independence. While Teacher is busy, the children learn independence, helping others and helping themselves. And the kids do learn to read, write and figure, don't they?

The answer, of course, is "Yes, they do." But not as well. A Wisconsin superintendent of schools reluctantly and secretively admitted to me that children who graduate from a one-room school average a year and a half lower in standard achievement tests than children from larger schools. Yet their I Qs are about equal. This finding was even more solidly established in a statewide survey by Burton W. Kreitlow, a farm education specialist of the University of Wisconsin.

I asked the superintendent why he doesn't show this fact

to farmers who vote to retain small country schools. "It's not what they want to hear," he said uncomfortably. "Remember that many of these people did not grow up in an educational tradition. They survived by hard work, not book learning. If someone like me says the country school isn't good enough, the farmer just grumbles, 'Well, you can't prove it.' I want to say, 'We can.' But the farmer has already turned around and walked away."

Bad schools have a tendency to get worse. A young father in the Ozarks, concerned for the education of his two children, explained to me, "With the young people around here gone, looking for work elsewhere, fewer kids get born, so state aid to schools keeps going down. A couple of years ago our school had to drop music and industrial arts. Before that, we lost our science teacher. The state law requires the teaching of science, so our kids had to take it by correspondence course."

Such schools will continue to get worse—and the real farm problem, a surplus of uneducated people, will intensify—unless Congress permits federal aid to equalize the opportunities of all children to go to a good school. Yet federal aid to schools is most consistently opposed by congressmen from the South and from prosperous farm areas, who eagerly vote billions for price supports that offer no ultimate solution to the farmers' problem. Rural congressmen are also the most active in blocking bills to train the needy for skilled jobs, even though a great proportion of these needy are farmers driven from the land, desperate to restore self-reliance and self-respect. Congress has yet to vote a billion dollars a year for retraining the unemployed, although it spends six billions a year to keep prices high.

To know the future of today's farm family, one must ask what will happen to the 1.5 million boys between the ages of ten and nineteen who today are growing up on farms. Only 150,000—one in ten—are expected to take over their fathers' land. Where are the others to go? What will they do?

The great, hopeful, surprisingly obvious but widely ignored fact is that their country sorely needs them—if they become educated, if their schoolteachers spur them to want to go to college. Great companies serving the modern farmer—makers of animal feeds, chemical fertilizers, farm machines—are pleading for trained workers and professionals. In city and country alike, the list of unfilled jobs for the skilled seems to grow at least as fast as the rolls of the unskilled unemployed. Recently California Polytechnic Institute at Pomona was dismayed to discover it was turning out only one agricultural school graduate for every six of its job opportunities. The Institute's San Luis Obispo campus, after placing all its graduates, had still not filled 150 jobs in agricultural management, processing, sales, finance, government, even some desirable foreign assignments. "Some of these unfilled jobs," said disappointed Warren T. Smith, dean of agriculture, "had salaries as high as $10,000 a year."

The new student of farming, entering a world of science and social relationships, must be not only better trained, but better rounded. Technology as a liberalizing force is reflected in a massive shift by agricultural colleges to emphasizing the humanities. Purdue University's "ag" school, which has increased minimum requirements in math, economics, and government from three hours each to six, also increased English and communications from nine to fifteen hours; it now encourages as much as six hours in a foreign language. Ohio State requires fifteen hours each of humanities, social sciences, and physical sciences.

Cultivation of educated men and women seems to be a farm program that cannot produce a surplus. A major national drive for a first-class education for all farm children—and job training for any surplus farmer who needs it—will establish a new kind of independence: the independence of men who are free to choose, who never become trapped into having to ask, "Where will I go? What will I do?"

7

towns without jobs

      If poor schools in poor farm areas tend to grow poorer, there are schools in poor coal mining areas of West Virginia and Kentucky that could hardly grow poorer without falling upon the heads of their pupils. They seem even too poor to be helped. In 1962 the federal government tried to guarantee that each of these schools should receive food to distribute for hot lunches. The plan failed because too many of the one-room schools lacked running water and electricity.

      Homer Bigart of *The New York Times*, in a memorable piece published October 20, 1963, describes a tour of Kentucky coal-town schools escorted by Leslie County Judge George Wooton:

      "At Gilbert's Creek, Judge Wooton stopped at a tar-

paper shack that looked like an abandoned farm shed.
Seven children were sitting at desks outside, taking
advantage of the Indian-summer sun. Their teacher, Mrs.
Ruth Stone, said she had moved them outside because the
shack was chilly and damp.

"The interior of the school was unfit for cattle. Daylight
shone through gaping holes between rotted planks; most
of the tar paper on the outside was missing. There was a
hole in the roof where the stovepipe should have been.

"Mrs. Stone said she could not light a fire because the
pipe was missing. The stove was so badly cracked she was
afraid to use it. Fortunately, the days had been warm, but
cold weather was imminent.

"The teacher had boarded up a hole under the stoop so
that any snakes there would not menace the pupils.

" 'I hear they're going to close the school and consolidate
us,' she said hopefully.

" 'Honey, they been saying that for ten years,' replied
Judge Wooton. The road to Gilbert's Creek is so bad, he
explained, that school buses could not reach the settlement
and bring the children to a consolidated school.

"Mrs. Stone, on the verge of tears, pleaded for a new
stove and some tar paper."

In nearby Letcher County, Dr. Randall D. Collins,
county health officer, said, "I've seen children who are
potbellied and anemic. I've seen children eat dirt out of
chimneys. Of 8,200 children in Letcher County, 75 to 85
per cent are underweight." Dr. Mary P. Fox, health officer
for Leslie and Knott counties, added that 75 per cent of the
children had intestinal parasites. In the village of Stinnett,
one child in ten has hookworm.

Benighted children rapidly grow into benighted adults.
In fourteen counties of eastern Kentucky, about 30 per
cent of the adults are functional illiterates. (Judging by

the Chicago experience, a far greater number can be
assumed to be occupationally illiterate.) Many of these are
young people in their teens and twenties, recent school
dropouts.

A limited skirmish against adult illiteracy is being
undertaken, not by the creaking, impoverished school
system (which spawned the illiteracy), but by a phil-
anthropic organization, the Council of the Southern
Mountains. At a recent meeting of the Council, Harry M.
Caudill, a Whitesburg, Kentucky, lawyer, and author of
Night Comes to the Cumberlands, a penetrating study of
the region, described how poverty and ignorance has fed
the growth of local political dynasties.

"The massive doling out of federal welfare money," he
pointed out, "has financed, and now sustains, a dozen or
more crafty, amoral, merciless and highly effective county-
wide political machines. They thrive on the present
economic malaise and are powerful because the people are
helpless. The continuance of their influence hinges on the
bloated welfare program, and they will oppose by every
available means any effort to restore the people to
productivity and self-reliance."

The leader of what has been called the state's strongest
political dynasty is Mrs. Marie Turner, administrator of a
powerful payroll as superintendent of schools in Breathitt
County. Mrs. Turner feelingly told Homer Bigart that,
despite the 75 per cent unemployment in her county, she
opposed efforts to invite factories into the area to provide
jobs.

"I'd hate to see industry come into our county," she said.
"People who go to factories lose contact with their
families. Those who stay home rear children who are pure
in thought."

She expressed gratitude that the county had "almost no

juvenile delinquency" and repeated, "I don't want to see factories."

While local politicians block jobs from coming in, federal politicians fail to encourage the unemployed to go out. Congress passed President Kennedy's area redevelopment and manpower training bills only after knocking out provisions that would have paid the transportation and temporary housing of unemployed families relocating where job opportunities are brighter. Local businessmen, who usually are the greatest influence on congressmen, are not about to support the depletion of their own customers and turn away the small but steady purchasing power of all those welfare checks. Furthermore, congressmen have little inclination to reduce the population of their districts, which might threaten the existence of their own seats. Without the votes of congressmen from such impoverished areas the bills had no hope of passage, so the Administration was forced to abandon its request for funds to relocate families. (Finally, in 1964, Congress gingerly permitted manpower officials to make some experimental studies in relocation.)

Why don't people get up and go for themselves? Many, of course, do. Coal-mining areas have sustained a great shrinkage of population. Some ex-miners find jobs, others contribute to the expansion of welfare rolls in larger cities. But most stay behind, victims of a cultural system of isolation, fear of the unfamiliar ways of the "outside" world, and, most entrapping of all, a deeply ingrained passivity and helplessness.

A man does not spend all of his working days in damp darkness, hammering and shoveling sludgy black rock, yet come out an adventure-minded man. Most of his intellectual powers must go toward the discipline of accepting his dull, dank existence without questioning, without wondering, without the upsetting influence of ambition. To live, one's ambitions must die.

In the early days, the mining companies enforced a rigid paternalism that solidified the miner's helplessness and dependence. Companies owned not only the mines, but often the miners' houses and even the stores in which they spent their meager pay checks. When a man's pay check ran out, company stores willingly extended a modest amount of credit; a miner in debt to the coal company was thus chained to his job, to his low wages, his company house, the high-priced company store. This practice gave rise to a miner's folk song which inscrutably became popular among urban teenagers a few years ago:

> *You load sixteen tons, what do you get?*
> *Another day older and deeper in debt.*
> *St. Peter, don't you call me 'cause I can't go,*
> *I owe my soul to the company store.*

The unions came to rescue the miner from all this. And the unions largely succeeded. Wages were lifted beyond those of most other laborers. Safety became a matter of importance. Exploitation at the company stores was checked. The old paternalism of the companies was smashed—and a brand new paternalism of the union took its place.

Recently I talked with Rivers C. Jones, former secretary of Local 6004 of the United Mine Workers at Glen Rogers, West Virginia. Evidence of the astuteness of Mr. Jones is his election to office over many years in an almost all-white union local, even though he is a Negro. He is also a forthright and self-questioning man.

"At the time the union was at its height," he said, "I was very proud of the great things we were doing for the men. But after the bottom dropped out, I watched those men and their families and for the first time I began to wonder. I watched them get poorer and poorer, more and more degraded in their way of life, their children getting skinnier and sicker. Yet they stayed there in those old homes, waiting, asking why somebody doesn't do something, but completely unprepared to size up their own situations.

"Then I began to look over our history and think about why. For years, a miner had his union deduct four-fifty a month for medical care for his whole family. That was a great benefit. Instead of the constant sickness he had in the old days, now he had nothing to worry about—nothing at all to worry about. The union got him group life insurance, a burial fund, and provided him with a negotiated wage. If he had trouble with a foreman, he had a grievance committee that worried about it. In the company store, if the miner thought a mistake was made, he didn't worry. He took it up with the union, and they took the worry off his mind. If he was injured in the mine, no matter how it happened, the union furnished a lawyer. In an injury case, as far as the union was concerned, the miner was never wrong.

"When the mines began closing down, the people looked around asking what was going to be done. None of them had any answers. Hardly any seemed to feel it was their job to think very hard. Taking care of them had always been somebody else's job. When the government offered surplus food if somebody local would cart it in and distribute it, the union took care of that for years. I really had to wonder for the first time in my life how much a man is really helped when an organization—even his own organization that he helped build—does everything for him year after year, so that when trouble comes the man is entirely untrained to think for himself and help himself."

Unemployment around the coal mines is dramatic because it cripples whole communities. Also, extreme poverty among coal miners, even though no worse than extreme poverty among sharecroppers, lends itself better to publicity and compassion. Miners in West Virginia and Kentucky are mostly white Anglo-Saxon Protestants. Their raggedy children have blond hair, blue eyes, the bloodlines of our pioneer heroes and the surnames of our Presidents. Their inability to cope with urban habits and aspirations cannot be ascribed, with a contemptuous wave of the hand, to African ancestors or inborn laziness or preoccupation with sexual lust.

But to place the dramatics of coal-mining unemployment in its proper statistical perspective it should be realized that jobless coal miners—at present numbering about 70,000—compose a shade more than *only one per cent* of the nation's unemployed. If all the magnificent, automatic coal-digging devices were melted down tomorrow, and all the men replaced by them restored to their miserable underground jobs, national unemployment would be affected by only the smallest degree. In ten years, from 1950 to 1960, coal-mine employment diminished by about 300,000 jobs (from 517,000 to 207,-000). Railroad jobs shrank by a little more, 437,000, and textile mills by a little less, 265,000. These declines were gradual and most of the people are employed in other work.

But compared to these figures, agriculture suffered a massive deflation from 7,140,000 to 4,527,000 farmers, not counting their wives and youngsters who lent hands at the farm work. For every job that has disappeared from the mines or the railroads or the looms, *ten families* are dispossessed of the only kind of life they ever imagined, the isolated, nonorganization life of the farm. The most numerous are also the least prepared for a new life in town.

Poor farm areas and the regions that have relied on coal mining, railroad shops, and textile mills are bound together by an important common fact: their traffic is chiefly one way, outward bound. The flow of energetic minds, such as these melancholy places produce them, is one way—out. There are vast areas that don't reveal to the casual visitor how poor they are, yet they lie like tranquil, shallow lakes, stagnating. They are going nowhere. They have been stripped of people with the energy, the will, the knowledge, to try leading them anywhere. To understand modern unemployment in the cities, we must understand the semirural towns that export the unemployed, and the look and feel of life in those places.

On the wall of the Washington office of William L. Batt, Jr., a tall, muscular, boyish-faced economic worrier for the federal government, there hangs a large white map of the United States splotched with patches of somber red. As he talks with visitors, Batt's eyes focus on one red splotch or another.

The dominant, dull white stretches of map describe affluent America—rich farm lands, booming cities, green-lawned suburbs, free-spending resort areas, the grand sweep of cornstalks and smokestacks, cattle and computers, that support Americans with more jobs, more money, more of that heady thing called prosperity, than the last generation of Americans ever dreamed they'd live to see. The red patches, however, mark those counties that were bypassed in the great coast-to-coast spill of prosperity. They are places of little cheer and deep trouble. And their number is great. Of 3,100 counties in affluent America, more than one in three—1,100 counties in all—have been designated by the Area Redevelopment Administration, the federal agency headed by Batt, as areas of "substantial and persistent unemployment for an extended period of time."

These regions are known in casual conversation as "depressed areas." But Batt and his colleagues wince at that term. They feel it is defeatist—in fact, depressing. Local folks resent it. So by law the areas are gingerly called "designated."

There are red pockmarks of designation in New England, fair-sized blots in upstate New York. A wide swath of red almost obliterates Pennsylvania, West Virginia, southern Ohio, western and southern Kentucky, and spills into Tennessee. All through the Old South there are as many globs of red as white, hopscotching to a solid wall of red in eastern Texas and Oklahoma. New Mexico is more red than white, and there is a huge spatter across Washington, Idaho, and Montana. Every square inch of Alaska is red and so is the island of Hawaii. Red spills across northern Minnesota, Wisconsin, and Michigan.

When I visited Batt, the red that most engaged our attention was a prodigious blot that covered thirty counties of southern Illinois, a most designated of designated areas. Those counties contain a remarkable mixture of almost every style of modern unemployment. Small farmers try to scratch a living out of eroded land, seeking part-time jobs in town but seldom finding them. Coal miners are reduced to relying on "rocking-chair money"—unemployment compensation—while an empire of coal lies beneath the earth, dug by more and more machines for fewer and fewer customers. Diggers of precious fluorspar along the banks of the Ohio River have been idle since Mexico captured much of the market with lower prices. In Mount Vernon a huge shop which once made freight cars is shut down for want of customers. As in many semirural areas, light industry has moved in to hire unskilled but eager hands for repetitive labor. Wages are low; if workers press hard for more money, machines may be installed to perform the simple drudgery faster, cheaper, and better.

"The region is loaded with manpower, minerals, and rivers waiting to be reorganized for new industries," Batt said, glaring at the red patch on his wall map. "And now capital can be lent under the Area Redevelopment Act. The only big shortage is in imaginative, experienced leadership—what I call 'local entrepreneurship.' But it's a resource that can be developed. There's more moxie in those towns than some people think."

Hours later my plane landed at Marion, Illinois, and in a rented car I headed north for West Frankfort, which Congressman Kenneth J. Gray, who represents most of the designated area, had told me was a town in deepest trouble. Until the end of World War II more than 10,000 coal miners thrived in its immediate environs—Franklin County. When I visited, only 817 were still clinging to their jobs. In two decades 40 per cent of the county's population has drifted away. One of every five of the remaining workers is unemployed. Almost 2,000 subsist on unemployment compensation, but more than 3,500 persons are supported by direct relief at a cost of $1.5 million a year—for one county. The total drainage on the state treasury for direct relief in southern Illinois is more than $30 million a year. Relief saps a staggering 20 per cent of the state budget.

About halfway to West Frankfort I slowed down at Johnston City, a coal town that is digging almost no coal. In anticipation of driving down the main drag, I conjured ancient images: breadlines, raggedy kids, mass fear on unshaven, gaunt faces—the look of the Great Depression. Then the images vanished; none of them seemed to fit what I saw. The mood of a depression—if Johnston City's trouble may be called a depression—is far different from the days of N R A, W P A, C C C. Parking places in Johnston City are hard to find; the streets are busy with polished, if not late-model, cars. Mothers pushing baby strollers chat earnestly, stopping to look in store windows. Teen-age girls, crisp and fetching in gay Capri pants, peruse photos in front of the Palace Theater. Under a neon sign, "Goodman Auto Sales," a window is emblazoned with large painted letters: "Business is GOOD."

I got out of the car for a closer look. Goodman Auto Sales had no autos on display. The showroom was cluttered with secondhand furniture and chipped enamel washers, bargains all. Mr. Goodman long ago had left with the last of his autos. Across the street the J C Roller Rink was closed. The Palace Theater was open Friday and Saturday nights only; the coming attraction was Gina Lollobrigida in *Go Naked in the World*.

In West Frankfort the economic distress is even more admirably concealed under a thin film of affluence. Solid old homes, many freshly painted, are ringed with flower gardens. Barker's Rexall Drug Store was atwitter with flapping banners heralding a one-cent sale in its sleek, self-service interior. The Fashion Shop was featuring a window display of gold slippers from $5.95 to $16.95. The Strand Theater, open seven nights a week, was showing—a return engagement by popular demand—*Breakfast at Tiffany's*.

"What got everybody here was things were sliding downhill a long time and nobody realized it," a red-haired policeman told me. He was slowly stirring a cup of coffee in an air-cooled café, in no hurry to get back into the hot sun. "They all bought little boats on payments. Then come a layoff in the mine, company shut down here, maybe open somewheres else, and a heapa boats in folks' backyards went on sale cheap. Ain't nobody buying though. But ain't nobody hungry either. It's just not like that."

During the glacially slow shift to a new economy of light industry, rocking-chair money has helped wall off the terror of the thirties. But the striking change from the panicky Great Depression of the thirties to the calm, composed Great Designation of the sixties is not so much in the composure of its victims as in who the victims are. In the thirties college men were forced into jobs digging ditches; the great national tragedy was waste of talent and skill. Today the tragedy is reversed. The ditchdigger—or his cousin, the pick-and-shovel miner—is rebuffed at every turn, for he has no school-learned skill to sell. Jobs need men, and men need jobs, but the men are insufficiently qualified.

"When I lose a mechanic or a salesman, it's a blow," said Clyde Brewster, a Ford dealer in Herrin. "The good men already have jobs."

"If I had five combination pipefitter-millwrights," said Link Perrin, manager of Herrin's state employment-service office, "I could place them in good jobs this afternoon. I have five jobs waiting for experienced secretaries, but nobody who can fill them."

Allen Industries in Herrin needed twenty power-sewing-machine operators to stitch auto upholstery; West Frankfort Apparel Company needed sixty operators. Neither company would risk a large-scale training program, for each operator costs $1,100 to train, and many applicants don't pan out. So the firms take on apprentices cautiously, two or three at a time. Those waiting their turn for a tryout, instead of being upgraded to taxpayers, remain as collectors of rocking-chair money. There's nothing else for them to do.

Meanwhile, high-school youngsters collect their diplomas, bid their parents and friends good-bye, then vanish. Some go to college, but many join the armed services or head for cities where job chances are brighter. Goffrey Hughes, former school superintendent of West Frankfort who became director of Southern Illinois, Inc., a regional chamber of commerce, was anguished by this exodus. "A farmer gets disturbed when his topsoil washes down the river," Hughes said. "He calls that soil erosion. Well, we get disturbed by the erosion of our finest high-school graduates when we desperately need them for future leaders. And we also need educated outsiders coming in, not only for their dollars, but for their culture and know-how. The traffic of good, energetic minds has all been one way—outward bound—and we've got to reverse it."

Even the exodus of manual workers is a skimming of cream. The best are first to go. Most reluctant to leave are the elderly and the less aggressive, those who are fearful they may not make their way in strange, faraway cities.

"Where'm I gonna go?" asked Charles Tessoni, an unemployed miner in his middle forties, standing beside his picket-fenced white house in the coal-patch town of Freeman Spur, population 460. Tessoni is a town-board member, and police and fire chief, salaried at two dollars a month. "I never been anywheres else. See that brown-shingled house two doors down? I was born there. This little town's my home. For fifteen years I was roof-bolting in the mine—you know, hammering bolts into the coal up above so it don't cave in. Then they fixed it so's all the roof-bolting was done by two men and a machine. I was one of the best two bolters, so they put me on the machine. Then in March 1961 the layoff came. The town has changed. Used to be there was a ball game every Sunday. Now no more. All the young punks are gone."

"The pitiful case," said Link Perrin, the employment-service manager, "is the miner between fifty and sixty. At sixty, he becomes eligible for his mine-union pension, at sixty-two for Social Security. He can retire with self-respect. But in his fifties, after his unemployment compensation gives out, he's forced into taking relief. He's the most beat guy you ever saw—worked hard all his life and come to this."

The relief rolls are not known for breeding self-esteem or ambition. That sad fact became underlined in a conversation with Mrs. Hallie Parrish, a kindly, grand-motherly politician who, for more than twenty years, had been elected Republican town-board member and relief administrator of Carbondale. It is a formidable job, for relief—$50,000 a year, plus state funds—is the biggest item in the town budget. She administers relief as a benevolent matriarch.

"Let's call it general assistance instead of relief," she gently suggested to me. "I think it's a nicer word. I'm fond of my people and I fight for them whether they're worthy or not. Some give me Hail Columbia, but most say I'm just like a mother to them.

"I give them no cash whatsoever. The state supervisor gets after me for that, but I think it's better to just pay their bills. I tell them they're allowed to spend so much for this and that, and I give disbursing orders to the dealers. I wrote one up today, a family of five. There was $101 a month for food, $15 for rent, $3.20 for bottled gas. In the winter they get $8.70 a ton for coal, in severe weather, two tons a month. They get $3.05 for electricity, an extra dollar if they have an electric refrigerator, and $3.24 for water and sewers. There's a few here that I've paid for their first baby. Sometimes, before you know it, I've brought three or four of their babies into the world. I get a rate at the local hospital for my babies, only $50.

"I'm always afraid when a young man comes in for the first time—because it'll be easier for him to come again. We have some second- and third-generation people. When people get in a habit, they go in that same trend, don't you know."

Congressman Gray, who punctuates sentences with the phrase "Our potential's unlimited," predicts a high rate of employment in five to ten years. Gray, a former auctioneer and car salesman who wears a flowing bow tie and a pearl-buttoned jacket that is often rumpled after inordinately long, furious hours in his Washington office, is a fierce scrapper for public-works projects. His district is a grid-work of gleaming new roads, and he'd repave them all tomorrow if he could get the money, just to employ his constituents. His zeal has won him election as a Democrat for six terms in what used to be a Republican district.

But neither Gray nor any associated optimists think that the pump-priming of public works will restore prosperity to southern Illinois. They pin much of their hope on private business activity which they hope will spread out, like economic ripples, from the Area Redevelopment Act. The act allows the federal government to lend up to 65 per cent of the money needed to start new businesses or expand old ones, if they will provide new permanent jobs. It also pays for training workers for such new jobs. Prosperity hopes also ride on the massive Manpower Development and Training Act to teach new skills to unemployed workers, not necessarily for newly created jobs, but those for which there are known shortages of workers.

The Area Redevelopment Act helped southern Illinois soon after its passage in 1961. An expanding New York State firm, Technical Tape Corporation, was scouting for a Midwestern plant. Goffrey Hughes, the regional chamber-of-commerce man, escorted company officials through empty factory buildings in the area. Their eyes were caught by a roomy warehouse at Carbondale, abandoned by a grocery chain and given to the city. They could rent the empty building at low cost from the city, borrow from the A R A to improve it, and get an outright A R A grant to train workers. The company, impressed by the economic charms of a designated area, quickly sewed up the deal.

A R A made its first loan, $455,000, to outfit the tape factory. Robert Keith, plant manager, was astonished at the zest of the local labor force when the job was completed days ahead of schedule. Keith, like other new employers, was at first apprehensive of the area's violent labor history. A neighboring county came to be known as "Bloody Williamson" thirty years ago when miners of Herrin forced strikebreakers into a death march and killed a dozen of them. A new generation of labor leaders has devoted itself to living down this fearful history; their association of business agents belongs to the regional chamber of commerce, helping to woo new businesses.

By early 1964 Keith had added a wing to the plant with a second A R A loan and hired more than 400 workers, trained by Southern Illinois University's Vocational Training Institute.

"It would have taken us three years to get into full production if we had had to finance the training ourselves," said Keith, who adds that he normally opposes government intervention in private business. "The beauty of the A R A is that it's not a giveaway. We have to pay back every cent of the building loan with interest. The workers, trained by government grant, became taxpayers after twelve weeks of training."

The company's payroll is expected to yield $226,000 annually in income taxes and slash $96,000 from relief payments and $363,000 from rocking-chair money—a year-after-year benefit to the public of $685,000—all for two loans and a $300,000 training grant. These benefits may be more than doubled by the "ripple effect" of new jobs. The U. S. Chamber of Commerce estimates that for each new job created in industry, 1.7 new jobs are born in trades and services—store clerks, car mechanics, waitresses, traveling salesmen, and so forth.

The U. S. Corps of Engineers approved the building of a huge dam in Franklin County that will back up the Big Muddy River into a 25,000-acre reservoir to be called Rend Lake. A R A agreed to lend money for part of its cost. The lake will control floods, attract tourists for fishing, swimming, and camping, invite retired settlers, and offer a 99 billion-gallon reservoir to thirsty factories. Its supporters say that new factories built beside Rend Lake will provide 5,000 jobs.

The quest for industry can be overdone at a time when the national shift in jobs is away from the factory, in the opinion of Chester Townsend, a native who is A R A coordinator for southern Illinois. "Everybody wants smokestacks," he said, "but by putting their imagination to work some of these towns would see they could solve their problems without a single new factory."

His favorite example is the historic city of Cairo, which Townsend calls "the southernmost city of the North and the northernmost city of the South." It is farther south than Richmond, Virginia, and is adorned with ante-bellum architecture and fine ironwork. Standing on an observation platform at the tip of its delta, a visitor looks down upon the confluence of the muddy blue Mississippi River and the muddy red Ohio, watches river barges drift by, and may dream of the great side-wheelers of Mark Twain's day. Along the Ohio River levees one may still see the fat-link chains that fastened Civil War gunboats to the bank. He may see where Ulysses S. Grant, a newly appointed general, loaded 3,000 men on steamers and went on to win his first major engagement at Belmont, Missouri.

"The town oozes tradition," says Townsend, "and it can be one of the biggest tourist attractions in the country." He visualizes a major restoration on the scale of Williamsburg, Virginia. The nearby juncture of two interstate highways, soon to be opened, will put Cairo within four hours' drive of 30 million people with more time and money to spend every year. Leaders in town nod sympathetically, but are puzzled as to how to begin, and their thoughts go back to solving their severe economic distress with smokestacks.

Frank Kirk, regional director of the state Board of Economic Development, emphasizes the development of lakes and national forests as an "industry" which will boom in an increasingly automated world. "We have to find our solution, not by following one path, but by recognizing how several are converging right under our noses. People have more leisure than ever, better cars and better roads than ever, and more and more they crave the forests, the hunting and fishing we have so much of."

The phenomenal growth of Southern Illinois University at Carbondale, from 4,000 students to 12,000 in only nine years, has already stirred the region. Its sleek new buildings and the ferment of student life are an invitation to reach upward for advanced skills. University life—its

demand for services—has already sharply reduced unemployment around Carbondale.

But amidst the long-range hopes for the neighboring
regions lies the present urgent necessity for jobs, which for
the time being means the need for factories. Where, I
couldn't help wondering, is the homegrown "moxie" described by William Batt that will pull these factory jobs
out of thin air? Is there a success story in even one town to
justify his faith in the others?

I stumbled over entrepreneurship at work in the once-
sleepy town of Pinckneyville. One doesn't hear much
about Pinckneyville in neighboring towns because its
success is puzzling, almost embarrassing, to those that
have not done so well. Only four men in town (population
3,000) were on relief, none of them able-bodied. I went to
see Mayor William J. Cunningham, who runs an insurance
office opposite the county courthouse.

"About ten years ago," he reminisced, "a few of us
started feeling the rumble of trouble. Nothing to hit a
fellow between the eyes. After all, the largest commercial
strip mine in the world was going just two miles south of
us. We had 600 working miners in town, all spending in
the stores. But we began to see our young folks turned
away when they looked for work. We saw machines coming in, tearing up farms to open new mines. Agriculture
started going down, but mine jobs weren't opening up.
Well, you don't need a ouija board to see some things, you
just feel them. We weren't going to wait until we were
down on our bellies.

"A young optometrist, Allen Baker, had just opened a
practice here. I don't know why he picked us, except we
got a long suit on friendliness. With the rumbling going on,
he began speaking up in the Chamber of Commerce about
getting factories, and first thing you know he took a course

at the university in economic geography. Then he whipped up a bunch of us to buck an old guard in the chamber and started raising money to get a factory built. We had no idea who'd want it or what they'd make in it. But we contacted churches, the Lions, the Rotary, the Kiwanis. We called a big town meeting. Ministers and priests pitched on Sunday, saying if you contribute to the factory, you're contributing to your church because you're helping to save it.

"In three weeks we raised $105,000. We gave out *whif* notes—repayable *wh*en and *if* we got the money back. The unions donated a lot of labor to put the building up. I was out there driving a grader.

"Then we began the selling campaign. Doc Baker was the letter writer and finance man. Charlie Rowe, the town abstractor, talked tax angles. Vic Provart, the lumberman, talked building prices. Eddie Weithorn, the five-and-ten owner, was the enthusiast. He'd tell a prospect about our great fishing, even though Eddie never fished a day in his life. I talked utilities. We subscribed to papers as far east as Philadelphia, watching for a fellow who was expanding. If we read about a flood, we'd write letters saying we're on high ground. We promised everybody we're A-bomb-proof because there's nothing worth blowing up around here.

"Well, for two years we dickered and didn't sell. Finally a fellow from Brooklyn came out, company that makes My-T-Fine desserts, and they bought the building for $125,000. With all their machinery they only hired thirty people, but we could pay back all those *whif* notes from the sale price, keep a profit for the next building, and we were on our way."

The technique has been repeated relentlessly, borrowing money, building and selling a factory, paying back. A handsome industrial park outside Pinckneyville is now occupied by the My-T-Fine factory, a Decca Records plant (employing 250), Acme Timber Products, making staves for whisky barrels (100 workers), and Perry Metal Products (140). All that was accomplished before the A R A came into being.

The spirit of town-saving so infused the people that next they kicked in $210,000 in *whif* money in six days to finance the Perry plant. "By that time," says Cunningham, "we'd take loans only in multiples of a thousand dollars to make the bookkeeping easier."

There were two exceptions to the thousand-dollar rule, however, each of them illustrating a beginning of determined, youthful entrepreneurship. At a wiener-and-cornbread feast on the courthouse green to celebrate the drive, nine-year old Freddie Mathis took out $50 he had saved for a horse and pressed it into the hand of Charlie Rowe, the town abstractor.

Rowe refused it, trying to convince Freddie that the money wasn't needed. When Freddie insisted, Rowe suggested, "Well, how about $5?"

After some haggling, they settled on thirty. Freddie paraded through the green proudly wearing a big badge, "I Gave $30."

Soon Freddie's friend Buddy Day, admiring the badge, approached Rowe to contribute all the resources he could quickly muster—a single penny. The plan for simple bookkeeping fell to pieces right there. Says Rowe: "I wouldn't have turned down that penny if I had had to add $999.99 to it myself."

After building the Perry Plant, the campaign for new buildings halted, at least for the time being. The town was fresh out of unemployed. If you ask anyone in town what really got it all started, the answer is almost always, "Doc Baker, I guess." An energetic college man—even though, of all things, an optometrist—had bucked a one-way tide of traffic and moved in while it seemed everyone else with energy was moving out. The dramatic success of his small band of co-workers makes one wonder: Are so many towns down and out because automation stripped them of their last hope? Or because preautomation drudgery stripped their people of ambition, self-reliance, and the opportunity to learn how to grow with the progress of events around them?

8

teach thyself

After becoming convinced that an automated society must be a trained society, the reader, if he is like hundreds of people I have talked with across America, is both uplifted and downcast. Who would not be gladdened at the prospect of finally banishing mass ignorance? But judging by the persistence of ignorance all around us, are we really to believe that *everyone* is capable of being trained? Isn't it true that some people are just plain stupid?

Undoubtedly. But undoubtedly, too, we will always have some jobs for the stupid. The trouble with that question—as with so many questions about automation—is that it is born of fear, not of a sense of opportunity.

Why don't we ask instead, "Isn't it true that millions of people, enslaved by tasks fit for the stupid, were born fit

to become trained, cultivated, educated human beings?"
Perhaps we should ask, "Why have we permitted this
terrible waste?"

The answer to that uncomfortable question bring us
back to the first chapter: each society produces the people
it needs. People have fitted themselves to tasks for the
stupid because as a society we have not needed the average citizen to be cultivated.

"As far as the average citizen is concerned," says Peter
Drucker, "automation's greatest impact will not be on
production technologies and will not be on employment.
The greatest impact of automation will be on our
intellectual and cultural life. . . . A society in which
automation has become a governing concept of production
and distribution is, of necessity, an 'educated society.' It is
a society in which knowledge rather than man's animal
energy is the central resource. . . . For the first time in
human history this has made possible a society in which
everyone with the intellectual capacity to acquire knowledge can be given an advanced education. In the past,
where physical brawn or manual skill alone were productive, the number of people to whom a society could
afford to give an education was severely limited. For
earlier society (including the society in which the men
now fifty grew up) did not consider knowledge an
economic resource, let alone the central capital of the
economy. . . . We can, increasingly, not afford to leave
anyone uneducated who has the capacity to become a
knowledge worker."

This realization has led to what we enjoy calling "the
educational revolution." Principals' conferences, teacher
conventions, P T A meetings, the magazines, T V, all are
alive with modern catchwords, "advanced placement,"
"programed learning," "the new math," "team teaching,"

"nongraded classes," and, most imposing of all, "curriculum reevaluation."

At every hand we learn that Johnny, whose alleged inability to read preoccupied the nation a decade ago, suddenly appears far brighter than we thought. In an outburst of educational experiments, kindergartners are studying geometry—and learning it with less resistance than junior high schoolers. First-graders who seemingly can't read "Run, Dick, Run" do learn to read if the words are sophisticated enough to be worth reading. In Massachusetts, third-graders study the nature of gases, comparative densities of matter, use of scientific measuring instruments. In Elkhart, Indiana, first-graders are captivated by a course in economics: the laws of supply and demand, economic geography, how a monetary system works.

Foundations have poured millions into developing these new elementary teaching programs, engaging such eminent scholars as Harvard's Jerome S. Bruner, Cornell's Philip Morrison, M I T's Jerrold Zacharias, and Purdue's Lawrence Senesh. These men have tried their revolutionary courses on children and they work.

But then the courses are transplanted from experimental classes to whole schools and suddenly they don't work any more. "The children aren't interested," teachers report. The scholars move in to investigate and find a strange thing: the children were ready to learn but the teachers were not ready to teach. Many teachers who have drilled class after class in memorizing multiplication tables don't really understand the underlying principles of mathematics. A great proportion of teachers, blinded to the principles of science by bad teaching when they were grade schoolers, are unable to teach others what they do not themselves understand. How can a teacher fascinate children with

economics when her own high-school classes convinced
her that it is a subject impossible of comprehension?

So we hear from every side that teacher-training institutions are useless. A more truthful statement is that, while
the needs of education have vastly changed, the method of
educating educators has not. Teachers are still being
trained for the needs of yesterday, when the aim of a
school was to "instruct"—to tell—a future citizen to
memorize certain facts, follow certain rules of discipline,
observe good habits, obey authority (in the person of the
teacher), and not to stray too far intellectually from the
group (if you go ahead too fast you'll be bored; fall
behind, you'll be "dumb"). The development of curiosity,
except in mild forms, has not been a goal of our schools.
After all, how is a teacher to *control* a classroom when
thirty-five untamed curiosities are running around loose?

The new importance of curiosity has not yet engaged
educators in great numbers. To most who are going along
with the "educational revolution," the new methods of
teaching are so many "tools" for speeding up old ways of
instruction. They seem to see the revolution as a great
efficiency program to deliver a bigger educational value
for the taxpayer's dollar. This is not the aim that Bruner,
Morrison, Zacharias, Senesh, and their colleagues have in
mind. They are trying to break away from an emphasis on
data and techniques, and replace it with an emphasis
on children *wondering why and how,* on *reasoning,* on
learning how things work—by sharpening the blades of
curiosity. In so doing, they are trying to enlist the schools
in creating a nation of people that can never again become
obsolete, of men that John W. Gardner calls "self-renewing."

"The self-renewing man," writes Gardner, president of
the Carnegie Foundation for the Advancement of Learn-

ing, "is versatile and adaptive. He is not trapped in the techniques, procedures, or routines of the moment. He is not the victim of fixed habits and attitudes. He is not imprisoned by extreme specialization. . . . We are beginning to understand how to educate for versatility and renewal, but we must deepen that understanding. If we indoctrinate the young person in an elaborate set of fixed beliefs, we are ensuring his early obsolescence. The alternative is to develop skills, attitudes, habits of mind, and the kinds of knowledge and understanding that will be instruments of continuous change and growth on the part of the young person. Then we shall have fashioned *a system that provides for its own continuous renewal.*"

In practical terms, what is meant by educating for the development of curiosity? Of numerous methods, let's look at one example.

At an extraordinary private school in Santa Monica, California, nobody was surprised when young Paul Schechter left for home at the end of a school day chatting excitedly about characteristics of triangles, squares, and circles. But at home his mother was surprised, and so was his father, Dr. Marshall Schechter, a psychiatrist and authority on child development. The subject struck them as unusually sophisticated for a child who was only three years old.

Nobody at the school ever is surprised when a four-year-old does arithmetic, including multiplying and dividing. There's mild surprise if a five-year-old *doesn't* read and write. Nobody is surprised when a six-year-old, picked from a class at random, is asked to explain square and cube roots —and does. I asked one, and the boy eagerly demonstrated by stringing lovely glass beads into rows of seven. He tied seven rows together into a square mat, then piled such mats seven deep and sewed them together into a cube. He looked at me searchingly to make sure I knew what was going on. Then he announced that he had assembled 343 beads—seven times seven times seven—so that, clearly, the cube of seven is 343 and the cube root of 343 is seven. "Are you sure you see?" he asked anxiously. Nobody would have been too surprised if the six-year-old had asked me in French. Seven-year-olds at the school often converse in French.

More surprising than any of these accomplishments are the I Qs of these children. They are not at all special. Their range is as wide as that of any ordinary school, from a dull 80 to a geniuslike 172.

This remarkable school is run—and here is the really disconcerting fact—by a handsome young couple, Tom and Delores Laughlin, who, before starting it four years ago, had never spent a day of their lives in the formal study of education. He was an ex-football star and moderately successful as a tough-guy actor for movies and T V; she had majored in art at college.

Are they intuitive geniuses at discovering new paths to the mysterious minds of children? Nothing of the kind. The Laughlins' school faithfully follows a plan of education, called the Montessori Method, developed and elaborately described half a century ago by an Italian woman physician, Dr. Maria Montessori. The system is widely practiced in Europe and parts of Asia, yet despite a great wave of interest here during World War I it did not take firm root in the schools of the United States. But in the past four years more than fifty private schools devoted to the radical methods of Maria Montessori have opened around the country. A landmark was reached in 1964 when for the first time a public-school system, that of New Rochelle, New York, decided to experiment with Montessori-style classes for preschool children of impoverished, educationally deprived families.

"What the Montessori Method says," according to Dr. Schechter, the psychiatrist who has two children of his own in the Laughlins' school, "is that you are permitted to be fully curious about a subject that interests you. But as soon as something interferes with your curiosity, you may shift to another subject until your curiosity in the first one returns.

"Curiosity is like a magnet that draws full attention. It creates the moments when people really learn. Usually we listen with half an ear. But if we're curious, everything opens up. We apply all our perceptions. We're really alive."

In years of experimentation, Dr. Montessori found that during the preschool years of three to six the child undergoes periods of special curiosity for certain kinds of learning. First the child is especially eager to master precise movement and coordination; by the age of four, this special sensitivity passes in most children. From about the third birthday to the sixth, the child is especially observant of how people behave—what might be called the social graces—and wants to learn to do the same; then that desire, if not satisfied, subsides. At the end of the third year and early in the fourth, most children seem especially susceptible to learning control of a pencil; they want to write words, then want to learn to read them, and finally become fascinated with numbers. All this before the fifth birthday.

These marvelous inner demands flower in a child precisely during the years—three to six—when we customarily give him the least opportunity, the fewest tools, the greatest absence of discipline and direction to help him in his quest to develop himself. We start him in school just as his

period of highest absorbency ends, after his preschool
environment has already helped him build a structure of
carefreeness, aimlessness, dependency on adults.

Dr. Montessori developed what she called a "prepared
environment" for the self-development of the preschooler,
as well as for the grade-schooler and high-schooler. For the
early years, the "prepared environment" is a roomful of
objects to bring the child tangible, concrete experiences—
not abstract lessons—for feeling, seeing, hearing, the
realities of language, numbers, music, geography, color,
design, geometric shapes. To instill self-confidence in a
world of daily practicalities, Montessori children are responsible for the orderliness of their classroom, serving
their lunches and cleaning up afterwards. The method's
emphasis on self-disciplined learning-how-to-learn, not on
adjustment to the ways of the group, is one of the main
ways Montessori differs from American brands of "pro-
gressive" education.

At the school run by the Laughlins (or any Montessori
school), one of the first objects that attracts a three-year-
old is a collection of colored geometric shapes arranged
like jigsaw puzzles in trays. Fitting the shapes into place
absorbs the child for a time, but then he wants to move to
something else. Soon he is fascinated by the feel and shape
of sandpaper-covered objects in the shape of letters. The
teacher teaches the child to recite a sound to identify each
—"puh" for *p*, "ih" for *i*, "nnnh" for *n*. Thus, at a time when
learning through the fingers is a fascination to the child, he
learns what letters mean and how they are shaped—the
elements of penmanship. Soon the teacher reveals how
they are combined magically into familiar words—"puh,
ih, nnnh—*pin!*" Next his interest in writing them awakens;
then, usually in the fifth year, an explosion of interest in
reading, the recognition of words he did not write. (Con-

ventional schools ignore the child's natural inclination to start by writing, and teach reading—the recognition of someone else's words—first.)

Sometimes before turning to letters, the child is captivated by devices that help him learn what numbers mean. Sometimes he works at them with a companion, sometimes with a group, sometimes alone. The teacher seems almost absent, yet she is ever-present, guiding children from one activity to another, making sure a child is ready for what he undertakes, helping children learn the experience of success, steering them away from failure. By experimentation, Dr. Montessori found that the pupil:teacher ratio for maximum learning under her self-teaching method should be an astonishing 40:1. If classes are smaller, the child tends to rely more heavily on the teacher's availability—and learns less.

One teacher, Teresa Egan, from Galway, Ireland, tells of one of her first pupils at the Laughlins' school, a boy whose lack of interest in reading caused his parents to fret. The child had learned to identify the sandpaper letters by sound, but did not move on to build words from them. His mind seemed always on geography. He spent hours on jigsaw map puzzles, colored flags that identified rivers, countries, capital cities, national styles of clothing.

The boy's mother began to protest. Why wasn't he reading? Why didn't he know arithmetic like others of his age in the class? The teacher patiently explained that his interests had not yet taken him there, but surely they would. What the child was learning—and geography would help him as well as arithmetic—was *how to learn,* the discipline of sustained interest. When the mother remained dissatisfied, the teacher felt obliged to protest that, after all, *the child was only four years old.*

Then one day, sitting with a box of sandpaper letters,

the child asked Miss Egan to help him sound out the names of countries. Leaping past the monosyllabic words, "cat," "run," "pen," he learned to spell the names of places that had long fascinated him. Then he became absorbed in writing them. This brought him to the enchantment of reading books about places; only pictures had attracted him before. When he discovered the marvel of stories, he dropped geography altogether. Soon he was taken up with numbers, growingly interested in anything that suggested a methodical system. One joy of discovery followed another.

The boy still had not arrived at his sixth birthday.

"The main difference between this school and regular school," said one qualified authority, an eleven-year-old girl who had transferred to a Montessori class from "regular" school, "is that in my old school they always made you memorize things and review them and all that. Here they let you *learn* them."

One American high school, perhaps more than any other, seems to have harnessed curiosity as a method for mass development of good minds for the new age. Jerome Bruner has described the high school of Melbourne, Florida, near Cape Kennedy, as one "that has changed the atmosphere of learning to conform to the spirit of the new curricula."

This historic change began unexpectedly one day when Dr. B. Frank Brown, the principal—fortyish, curly-haired, bony-jawed—leaned back in his swivel chair to hear out a problem of the most popular and influential senior in school, seventeen-year-old Bill Nelson. The youngster had just been elected president of the Key Club International, a high-school-student version of the Kiwanis, and was receiving invitations from schools all over the country to make speeches. The experience would be very valuable, but he'd also have to miss school for days on end. If he were permitted to accept the invitation, Bill pleaded, he'd use the long hours on trains and planes to study. By seeing his teachers privately before each trip to get assignments, and after each trip to take tests, he was sure he could keep up with his studies.

It was a very irregular request. But Brown, himself the product of a bizarre history as a student, recently had made up his mind that the nation's schools, as well as his own, were entirely too regular. They marched boys and girls toward diplomas in lockstep conformity, although the youngsters' ambitions and abilities were shaped and colored as differently as shells at Melbourne Beach. Bill Nelson had, after all, maintained an A average all through high school. Brown decided to let the boy go traveling.

Some weeks later, Brown checked with Bill's teachers and discovered that not only was Bill continuing to knock down A's on exams without the benefit of regular classroom instruction, but he seemed more interested in his school work than he had ever been. Unchained from the strict prescriptions of daily classes and homework, Bill's curiosity had begun to run loose. He was reading far more deeply into his subjects than he was required to do. Brown began to wonder if the classroom was really the best place for every student to be.

That was five years ago. Since then Melbourne High has been remolded by Brown into what many educators regard as one of the most exciting high schools in the United States.

"If a girl can learn more German by reading alone in the janitor's storage room, why keep her in a classroom?" Brown asks. That question is not hypothetical. Doris May Bennett, a pretty seventeen-year-old honor student, came

to Brown one day asking permission to drop her major
subject, German, in which she had been earning A's. She
was eager to read German poetry and plays, but she was
trapped in dull drill of grammar which she had already
mastered. Brown told Doris to stay away from the classroom except for exams. He gave her a corner of the
janitor's storage room, got her some books of German
poetry and plays, and arranged for Doris to meet her
teachers twice a week. Her interest in German soared.

Brown began taking applications from other ambitious
students who wished to pursue independent scholarship in
the janitor's storage room. The room soon became so
crowded that Brown expropriated it from the janitor and
tacked a sign on its locked door reading "Center for
Advanced Study." A key to the room is a badge of
membership in Melbourne High's most exclusive and re-
spected club. More than a hundred students out of an
enrollment of two thousand have been sprung from the
classroom of their best subject—in Brown's phrase they
have "escaped forward"—to enjoy the excitement of self-
propelled, self-reliant learning.

"The slowest student in this school as well as the
brightest one," says Brown, "is capable of things we never
dreamed he could do. But each is the prisoner of the other
in lockstep education."

The slowest students at Melbourne as well as the fastest
have indeed had their school lives changed by Brown's
unorthodoxy. Melbourne High is the only completely
nongraded high school in the United States. Before entering any new course of study, a student takes a standard
achievement test to measure what he already knows.
Regardless of his year in school, if he can pass first-year
chemistry without taking it, he doesn't waste his time taking it; instead he enrolls directly in second-year chemistry.

Before graduating, many "escape forward" into advanced college work.

On the other hand, a student is not forced to batter his head in a losing battle against Shakespeare if he hasn't learned to read properly.

I talked to one seventeen-year-old boy who somehow was pushed upward out of grammar school almost unable to read. In one year, under specialized instruction, he progressed from a second-grade to a fifth-grade reader. For the first time, he was *enjoying* the struggle to make out the meanings of printed words. He no longer feels trapped among kids who are "smarter"; he is no longer the teacher's "problem" in a class analyzing Shakespeare. The same lad is a star student in the auto-repair shop and has been earning B's in senior algebra. In another school, he might be denied a diploma for failing to master Shakespeare, or teachers might be persuaded to drag him through just to get rid of him. At Melbourne, he earned his diploma honorably for passing all the subjects he was prepared to study.

Students in the great middle ground, too, pit themselves against each subject with an intensity gauged to keep them on their toes. They may choose a subject in any of five different "phases"—Brown's word for the scope of curiosity a course will try to satisfy. One student may choose Phase II (a cautious treading) in history, but Phase V (a blue-sky quest) in physics. Their choices must be approved by teachers, but so far, according to Brown, the students have proved reliable judges of their proper level of challenge.

When students enter Melbourne, they take a test in basic English—spelling, grammar, punctuation. If a student does poorly, he enters a class that concentrates on the mechanics of the language. If he gets a high score, he is never drilled in the mechanics again. Even then, he does not march lockstep with his peers through successive courses in English literature. At Melbourne, there is no such thing as sophomore, junior, and senior English. A student chooses a teacher instead of a course. One teacher is noted to be a live wire on Shakespeare, another on the modern novel. A student may choose them in any sequence he likes, but may not choose the same teacher twice. Thus Phase V sophomores, juniors, and seniors are in the same room ricocheting ideas off one another, while in another room Phase IIIs are doing the same. They are grouped as intellectual, not chronological, peers.

"Until you break up grades," says science teacher Gerald Einum, "you don't realize how futile it is to be teaching a group of kids the same material merely because they're the same age. Slow students and fast students live in separate worlds. Even the teacher doesn't know how different they are until he teaches them separately. We haven't begun to realize how imaginative the fast student can be—how much challenge he needs to keep him interested—and how much specialized help the slow student needs to keep him from closing his mind and quitting. I am constantly surprised in both directions."

Educators besiege Melbourne with visits to see what in the world is going on there. Landing at the same airfield that serves Cape Kennedy, they often assume that the school's science whiz-kids are missile-happy. It's a natural assumption. But of all the students freed from science classes for independent study, not one has undertaken a project connected with rocketry. Their preoccupation, as might be expected in a school near water, is marine biology. When I visited, Paul Kurek was perfecting a way to isolate and identify the hormones in the pituitary glands of frogs, employing equipment he designed himself. Joe

Brannon was working hard to discover how the sea anemone operates its poisonous sting. He was racing against a Japanese biology professor engaged in an almost identical quest. For six consecutive years Melbourne students had taken first prize in biology (but never in physics) at the state high-school science fair. Chris Cherniak removed the nerve fibers of a horseshoe crab and, six weeks after the death of the crab, Chris was transmitting electrochemical impulses from one disembodied nerve to another. Chris's project was awarded first prize—a $7,500 scholarship—over 23,000 entries by high-school seniors in the Westinghouse Science Talent Search.

Brown gets annoyed when visitors, seeking easy explanations for Melbourne's academic fervor, suggest, "Of course, this is a special community. You're so near Cape Kennedy. . . ." Brown acidly replies, "I believe the folks at the Cape would be doing what they're doing whether we were here or not." Then he points out that the school's I Q average is only two points above the national school average—frequently lower than that of the school whose principal is visiting.

"There are two ways to get to the top of an oak tree," Brown recently told a principals' convention. "Climb it or sit on an acorn. The conventional administrator has chosen to sit on an acorn. . . . The graded organization has never served the learning needs of children very well. It is in no way geared to the varying rates at which children learn. The modern goal of graded education is to remake everyone in the image of comfortable kids from suburbia. Teaching in graded schools is not a discipline at all. It is a moralistic effort to embourgeois.

"The result is a school-leaving problem which has become a national scandal."

At Melbourne, each year of nongrading resulted in further decreases in the number of dropouts. While the national dropout rate holds at 30 per cent, Melbourne's progressively dropped to a mere 4 per cent in 1963. As students were offered the initiative for their own education, their behavior almost immediately underwent a surprising transformation. At first, teachers were noticeably less needed for monitor duty in halls, the cafeteria, and bus-loading areas. Finally, Brown eliminated monitors —either teachers or students. By the middle of the third year of gradeless education, the school abandoned staff attention to truancy. The problem had eliminated itself. The job of dean of students had become transformed from one of administering discipline to counseling for advanced education and careers.

"There are still occasional discipline problems at Melbourne," says Brown, "but all of them originate in the classroom. The indication is strong that even these are generated by the teacher rather than the student."

Five years ago, when Brown's program was first taking shape, 40 per cent of Melbourne's graduates entered college; of the June 1963 graduating class, 73 per cent were accepted by colleges and universities offering four-year degrees. In 1961 and 1963, National Merit scholarships were won by Melbourne students. Brown gives out these figures with the misgivings of a soldier winning a medal for the wrong act of valor. "These are measures of achievement," he protests. "But the whole idea of our school is to cultivate imagination and creativity. These are often confused with achievement but are not the same thing. Einstein used to preach that imagination is far more important than knowledge, and that's our byword."

If a community expresses its sense of values by the leaders it elects, Melbourne High values the all-around achiever. At the time of my visit, its president of the student council was Clifton McClelland, like many school heroes an athlete, a seven-time starter for the football varsity. But the chief interests that preoccupied him—that really got him going in a conversation—were his self-propelled studies in mathematics in the janitor's storage room. His classroom work in math kept touching on wondrous phenomena, then switching too quickly to others. He wanted to look deeper before moving on. So Cliff designed a course for himself in the mathematics of probability, properties of numbers, and groups and fields —all advanced college work. "Right now," McClelland told me, "I'm interested in the derivatives of trigonometric functions. My teacher said she'd learned some of that in college, but she's forgotten it. So we're studying it together. After we go a certain distance, she makes up a test and gives it to me."

I asked teachers if their usually well-organized schedules don't get ruined by the demands of the students running off in independent directions of study. They all said, in tones of mild surprise, no.

"A teacher gets nervous but excited about getting a student in independent study," said Mrs. Inez Shirley, a math teacher. "I had two boys working on calculus, Brian Pierce and Ronnie Keiser, who were both also doing advanced independent study in physics. Their minds began to spark with relationships that they'd never be able to pursue in the classroom. They forced me to go into independent study of my own in physics. I'd see John Wessner, the physics teacher, coming down the hall and I'd say, 'Mr. Wessner, I need you.' And he'd say, 'I was looking for you too. Those boys are making me dig out my calculus again.' Some teachers might think this is harassing, but it's just what teaching has always needed, a generalizing of the sciences."

Just as students at Melbourne seem to be engaged in academic competition, so are the teachers. Priscilla Griffith, chairman of the history department, says, "Lots of kids go into science because that's where all the excitement seems to be. But they'd specialize in the humanities —history, English, economics—if schools got away from the old ways of laying out the answers cut and dried. Students want the excitement of conflicts in ideas, of searching for their own answers. They like problems that don't have a single answer but leave them puzzled among five or six."

A favorite teacher is Dr. MacClellan C. Fellows, who has spent a career not as a teacher but a dentist. For thirty years he practiced in China and spent two years during the Korean conflict in a Red prison camp. After his release he came to Melbourne to retire. Brown convinced Dr. Fellows to start teaching Chinese. (Doris May Bennett, in her second year of Chinese, said, wide-eyed, "It's easier than German.") Then Dr. Fellows launched a course in "The Culture and History of the Asian People." He could find no textbook to go by, so he wrote one, 150 pages long. A missile contractor, the Radiation Corporation, printed the book on its office duplicating machine. One night a month, Dr. Fellows's students gather in the home economics kitchen to cook an authentic Chinese meal, then eat it with chopsticks.

Recently Melbourne began to offer a course in classical Greek.

The jaws of visitors sag when they learn that Melbourne operates on a budget of $351 a year per student. The national average for high schools is about $390. The "better" schools spend more than $700. Melbourne's teachers carry the main burden of the tight budget; their salaries begin at only $4,100. Yet Brown gets applications from experienced teachers everywhere who hear of the academic excitement at Melbourne and are willing to sacrifice higher salaries for it. "I've never seen kids," says English teacher Barbara Bixby, "so highly motivated and purposeful. It's a constant surprise."

Brown, who battles for a higher budget on the one hand, finds ways of padding the earnings of teachers on the other. He keeps a constant correspondence seeking foundation grants and scholarships to finance his teachers' summer study. He is permitted to pay an extra stipend to a teacher who puts in extra hours as an athletic coach. Reading this rule broadly, he had made a "coach" of science teacher Gerald Einum. "Watch him in the lab with those youngsters any day after school," says Brown, "and you'll see the greatest coach you ever saw." Brown has also been known to dip his hand into the athletic fund to buy unprescribed textbooks for students in advanced study. The athletic coaches, as one athlete put it to me, "are not too happy with the academic bit." But they have produced championship teams.

When visitors point out a teaching technique they admire, Brown enjoys confounding them by saying, "Yes, but we're trying to make it obsolete. Every time we find a bright new heresy we try to make it obsolete before it becomes a dull new orthodoxy. Schools can't wait any more for time to change them. We have to take the lead in change if we're going to train youngsters to be leaders of change. Yet, look around our schools and you see the bland leading the bland. There's enough dead wood teaching in the schools of America to heat the schools of Wisconsin for a whole winter." When Brown fails to impress a visitor, he is sure to succeed in antagonizing him; Brown seems satisfied either way.

Although he was unaware of it at the time, Brown's heretical notions about schooling were born during his own student days in Dublin, Georgia, days that were so bland he has difficulty remembering his teachers' names, their faces, or what they taught him. In high school, he got poor grades and was, in teachers' parlance, a "chalk thrower." One night he climbed through the schoolhouse window, turned on all the bells and ran. They kept ringing until the janitor arrived. (Brown has taken no chances at Melbourne; he has installed a bell system that automatically shuts itself off.) In his senior year, Brown quit. It may come as a shock to Melbourne students to learn that their principal has never earned a high-school diploma.

After a spring and summer of boredom, Brown decided to give Young Harris Junior College an opportunity to interest him. He liked it immediately. Teachers called him Mr. Brown and expected him to be self-reliant. The transcript of his high-school record did not arrive until after the first college marking period, when he was already on the honor roll with an average of 98. Upon seeing his record, college officials demanded that Brown finish his high-school courses. But he argued back, "If I've already passed college math, why do you want me to waste my time with lower grade work?" The officials were disconcerted by this unorthodox idea, but after six months of haggling, Brown won. That was his first object lesson in nongraded schooling.

After earning his bachelor's degree at the University of Florida in 1938, Brown taught at the high school of Hohokus, New Jersey. The big educational sensation of that day—which later fizzled—was radio in the classroom. Every morning a program called "School of the Air" was imposed upon students. Everybody listened, it seemed, but few really learned. "Today," says Brown, "they're trying to put over television in the classroom. It's premature gadgetry. T V fixes the attention without engaging the mind. Frank Lloyd Wright called T V 'chewing gum for the eyes,' and I agree with him."

In 1950, married and a father, Brown decided to go after a Ph.D. at the University of Florida. For his dissertation he wrote an ambitious history of the twenty-five leading thinkers in education. His professors told him it was a fine job, but too big a subject for a Ph.D. candidate. Brown then examined subjects approved for other Ph. D. candidates. "It was easy to see they thrived on narrowness," Brown says. He chose a narrow subject concerning school superintendents in Florida, puffed it up to 160 pages, and earned his doctorate.

He was supervisory principal of a small school system in "the sweetest little town in the U. S. A.," the sugar-cane town of Clewiston, Florida, when he was asked to take over Melbourne High School in 1952.

"If I had known how bad things were at Melbourne, I wouldn't have come," Brown muses. Missile engineers were moving their families in by the hundreds and were dissatisfied with the schools. Committees of parents were roaming through the classrooms, then sending harsh reports to the newspapers. Brown was not unsympathetic with their aims, but he tried to persuade them that a good school doesn't grow in chaos. Teachers were so scared by the parent committees that their minds were diverted from their students. Three months after he arrived, Brown gave the parent committees an ultimatum: either he would run the school or they would. They withdrew and Brown soon began the innovations that were to prove so successful.

At educational conventions, Brown preaches nongraded

schooling, but has difficulty getting other principals to dare to try it themselves. One of the reasons, he believes, is that a disproportionate number of school administrators are former athletic coaches who are not really education-minded.

Recently, he was scheduled to address a morning session of a principals' convention at Detroit. From the rostrum he could hardly see his audience. Faces were concealed behind a wall of newspapers, open to the sports pages. He decided to extemporize an opening sentence. "Upgrading of education," he began, "will hasten the decline of varsity athletics." As though a fierce wind had blown through the hall, newspapers swished down, and popeyed faces leaned forward to catch his next words. Brown had won their attention. The more education-minded educators among them, in growing numbers, have been giving him a certain amount of attention ever since.

9

the new working class

America is witnessing the emergence of a new working class, a kind that Karl Marx hardly imagined. It is a working class of clean hands and trained minds, physical comfort and economic security, and, to varying degrees, a class of decision-makers instead of drudges.

Already the members of society that Peter F. Drucker, the New York University economist, calls "knowledge workers"—and the Census Bureau calls "technical, professional and managerial"—outnumber industrial production workers. In twenty years, Drucker forecasts, "knowledge workers" will constitute half the work force. If the definition of this category is expanded to include sales and clerical jobs, in twenty years three working Americans out of four will be "knowledge workers."

What kind of still-undisclosed life awaits this 1984 class of "knowledge workers," who unsuspectingly are now studying the three Rs in ordinary grammar-school classes? But even before looking into the lives of the new working class, let's see what has been happening to the old, familiar one. Let's leave aside all the sociological conjectures about the dire consequences of automation, and look at some actual numbers to see what has been happening to jobs in America.

Of the fifty-eight leading industries in the American economy, as compiled by Columbia University's Bureau of Applied Social Research, only four had a significant reduction of the number of their workers in the decade ending 1960: coal mining, textile mills, railroads, and the one that dwarfs the other three, agriculture.

The loss of 435,000 railroad jobs is more than offset by simultaneous gains in more up-to-date transportation. The making of airplanes added 410,000 workers from 1950 to 1960, and the running of commercial airlines grew by another 100,000. According to Columbia's economists, aircraft manufacture will zoom aloft with an additional 1 million workers by 1970.

The loss of 265,000 jobs in textile mills is more than offset by the gain in pleasanter jobs selling what the automated mills produce. Clothing- and general-merchandise-store employment has risen by 360,000 in a decade—in line with the national shift from manufacturing to service.

The loss of 310,000 jobs in coal mining is almost entirely offset by the manufacture of related products, petroleum and chemicals. These are supposed to be the most automated industries of all, yet their number of jobs has risen by 260,000 in a decade.

Almost the entire remainder of the list of fifty-eight

industries reveals growth, growth, growth. In many, the growth of jobs would be greater if there were trained people running loose who could fill the vacancies. Banking jobs, supposedly threatened by computers, burgeoned by 400,000 in a decade, and will add another 600,000 by 1970. Insurance companies, also big users of computers, added 300,000 employees from 1950 to 1960 and will have put on 400,000 more by 1970.

The growth is not all in white-collar wearers and graduates of academic courses of study. Workers in gasoline stations will have increased in two decades (1950–70) by 420,000; in clothing manufacturing by 225,000; in trucking and warehousing by 480,000; in wholesaling by 560,000; in fabricated metals by 700,000; in general machinery by 720,000; in electrical machinery by 1,200,000.

But as one reads down the list of numbers, one overwhelming loss seems to wipe out all the gains. There is the fearsome reduction of 3.6 million jobs in agriculture. What industry could possibly grow so big and so fast as to offset so mammoth a shrinkage in another?

Indeed there is one. It poetically symbolizes the profound change taking place between 1950 and 1970 in the organization and purposes of mankind. A two-decade estimated decline of 3.6 million toilers in the most ancient of occupations, farming, is precisely offset by a gain of 3.6 million in the most civilized of occupations, education. The cultural enrichment of one human being by another is rapidly becoming America's largest industry—and by 1985 it probably will be.

In a single generation we see a microcosm of all civilized history. Simultaneously we see the conversion of the children of food gatherers and mineral diggers to factory workers; of the children of factory workers to clerks, machinists, scientists, and managers; of the children of clerks, machinists, scientists, and managers to teachers. The meaning of "labor-saving" machines goes beyond creating more work than they eliminate. Machines change the work that man does.

But no matter how fast our imagination may run in visualizing this change, the change really happens more slowly than we imagine. There is a popular impression that the average factory worker, by pushing the buttons of a robot, will soon do the work that in the recent past required an army of manual workers. This groundless supposition leads to such panicky writings by otherwise levelheaded men as Donald Michael's *The Silent Conquest*.

The truth is that the rate of increase in productivity of an average factory worker is not speeding up, but has slowed to almost half of what it was forty years ago. In the 1920s, as Professor Yale Brozen of the University of Chicago points out, the rate of increase per man-hour was 5.3 per cent per year. From 1947 to 1953, the rate had slowed down to 3.2 per cent. Since 1953 it has dropped further to 2.7 per cent.

It's not that we don't know how to make automation move faster. John Goodell once remarked that he believes the only operative worker not replaceable by a machine is a barber. But know-how is far from enough. Cost is an almost unimaginably large obstacle. The more that machines replace men, the more expensive it becomes for additional, more specialized machines to replace additional, more specialized men. In the late 1940s the cost of replacing a single coal miner was about $20,000. The miner's union had driven wages up so high for common laborers ("Where else can I make thirteen-o-five a day?" asked the Centralia miner in 1947 when that was a formidable wage) that mine owners found it cheaper to mechanize. Now that mine employment is less than half what it was, the cost of replacing a man is more than twice as much, $50,000. Since it is now cheaper to pay wages than to mechanize, human employment is relatively stable.

Professor Brozen estimates that putting our present know-how into practice in factories alone, which now employ only about 25 per cent of American breadwinners, would cost a thousand times two and a half billion dollars —in astronomical shorthand, $2.5 trillion. The annual rate at which American companies are now able to invest in new plant and manufacturing equipment is a paltry $15 billion. At the current rate of conversion to new equipment, American factories could not be automated up to our present know-how for 200 years. At that, we would have kept pace only with present production of goods— not an extra T V set or ballpoint pen or sugared doughnut. If we tried to keep up with expanding demand of a growing and wealthier population, we could never catch up at all unless the cost of automation equipment were reduced to one-sixth of what it costs now. Even though the cost is declining, so great a slash is hardly a thinkable prospect for this generation.

A last word to quiet the alarmists: Even where jobs are eliminated from the modern factory, automation is not the biggest cause. Recently a McGraw-Hill trade magazine, *Factory*, surveyed 500 factories, large and small, to discover reasons for abolishing jobs. Only 16 per cent of doomed factory jobs were attributed to new machines. The biggest single cause, applying to 30 per cent of the cases, was elimination of waste in work methods—or just plain efficiency. In the office, where the computer has come to be regarded as a villain, only five per cent of job cuts were ascribed to the machine, 54 per cent to more efficient office routines.

If we are to maintain a national attitude of dreading new machines because they threaten obsolete jobs, we will be much more sensible to go out and campaign against the insidious threat of efficiency.

The new work of human beings is undergoing a profound change in function, parallel to the change in function of significant new machines—computers and robots alike. Human work is becoming less specialized, more convertible, more dependent on what is peculiarly human—the intellect.

To understand this development, let's take a new look at the TransfeRobot. Its inventor analyzed—and *generalized* —hundreds of diverse, time-consuming, repetitive human tasks down to a single, basic, common function: picking up and putting down. Almost the entire machine is engineered for that *general* use. A small part of it, its custom-designed "fingers," adapt the whole machine to the specific task at hand. Similarly, the computer is designed for the *general* use of containing facts—*any* facts—and pouring them back in assembled sets on command. For example, a computer in the employ of an airline will "remember" how many seats are available for what class of service for each of thousands of scheduled flights, revise its information each time a seat is sold or canceled, "remember" each passenger's name, his phone number, even his meal preferences on Friday. If a clerk erroneously records Mr. Glasgow as Mr. Blasgow, the computer will search its memory for a name that is something like Glasgow. But that's all part of one specialized task. The same computer can reassemble all that information into reports for top management on sales, passenger-load factors, and ratio of cost to income of every trip on each of the airline's routes. Then the computer can turn to entirely new collections of information, entirely new problems. It can make out the airline's payroll, including printing the individual pay checks, then accomplish the complex chore of scheduling work assignments for stewardesses (never forgetting the order in which each girl stated a preference for one route over another, and allowing each girl her beauty rest between trips).

By relieving men of the specialized tasks of being "experts" in mere information or mere administrative procedures, and relieving other men of specialized manual operations, new machines clear the way for mankind to practice a *generalized* skill: figuring out new things to be done, and how to do them. Man turns to pursuing his curiosity, analyzing, problem solving—the functions that only a human being can perform. His chief skill is the proper use of his analytical mind. A well-trained mind absorbs the specialized knowledge of a specialized task in a way that is similar to—although surely not as simple as—fitting a new set of fingers to a TransfeRobot.

A neighbor of mine recently provided me with a lucid illustration. He was employed by a firm that makes complex optical instruments and told me he was engaged in inventing a horizon scanner that would automatically steer space satellites. I remarked that I had been under the impression that his formal training was in mechanical engineering. It was, he said. But nobody in school had been trained to invent horizon scanners, nor for that matter to think seriously about space ships. These jobs are given today to men of basic training in *how things work*— almost any kind of engineers who have demonstrated their ability to figure out new things, evaluate them, and apply them. My neighbor was valuable to his company, not for the specialized information he brought—he could have learned that—but because he could think.

When information and computation are delegated to machines, and curiosity becomes the business of man, fantastic worlds open up. Fifteen years ago, when the computer, which has already changed the world, was just being born, experts predicted that a dozen computers placed strategically around the country would answer all the questions that curious Americans could conceivably ask. Today, more than 10,000 computers are in use and manufacturers cannot keep up with the demand for more. John Diebold, a pioneer automation consultant, predicts that by 1970 the telephone company will earn more from conversations between computers than conversations between people. (Doesn't that sound dreadful? All it means is that you are standing at an American Airlines desk at Kennedy Airport impatiently asking a clerk if you can get on the next flight to Chicago. Instead of the passenger agent picking up a telephone and waiting for someone at the other end who always seemed too busy to answer, now he inserts a card in a slot and instantly a green light flashes, which merely means that a machine in Briarcliff Manor, New York, said "Yes." Incidentally, as the convenience of air travel has increased, so has the number of passengers—and so has the number of jobs. And fares are going down, which may boost employment even more.)

Each revolutionary development that impresses us as the last word soon turns out to be merely one of the first. Edwin F. Shelley, who first described to John Goodell the need for a TransfeRobot, recently pointed out in a speech:

"The rise of the modern computer was really made possible by the development of a substitute for the vacuum tube, namely, the transistor, with its much higher reliability and much lower cost. But the transistor is just a way-station on a fantastic road which leads to the wonderful world of molecular electronics. In this world, both size and cost shrink by factors of thousands, and reliability approaches perfection. Computer elements in this world, for example, are not made up of resistors, capacitors, transistors, inductors, each of which has been separately manufactured and then assembled and wired. Instead, computer elements are made by rearranging the *molecules* of special materials to form the desired circuit patterns, and the entire computer-element assembly may be the size of a pinhead. The entire computer itself then approaches the dimensions of a carton of cigarettes—or of the human brain. No moving parts, no heat, no perceptible aging— just cold, solid, low-cost decision-making and control."

Mindful that the importance of a machine is its social consequences, Shelley comments:

"As a society, then, we have a choice. We can look ahead to the grim prospect of ever-increasing dislocation and unemployment, and reconcile ourselves to increasingly difficult measures to remedy the social consequences of this unemployment. Or we can seize the marvelous opportunity which automation presents to release the human race from the drudgery of machine-like tasks. We can devote the unlimited abundance which is available to us, for the first time in history, to the development of men's minds. In practical terms, we can now afford the time and effort to *educate* mankind, since it is no longer necessary to devote our resources solely to the production of our goods and services.

"And it is clear that in the new era of automation, a tremendous increase in education is both an economic and political necessity. All too many people . . . have no strong grounding in the physical or social sciences, or in the techniques of purposeful thinking and discovery. . . . If an economy is to use its people for human tasks rather than machine tasks, it must educate its people to versatility and to change. For both economic and political reasons, therefore, the breadth and depth of education must be expanded by an order of magnitude, and the philosophy of a continuing education throughout life, for every citizen, must be established."

What Shelley is describing is the need for the mass cultivation of educated, analytical, generalizing, multipurpose men for an age that has harnessed the use of general, multipurpose machines.

In the past we have not had general, multipurpose men in quantity because we have not needed them. Each society produces the men it needs. Alfred North Whitehead, the mathematician and philosopher, in *Science and the Modern World* points out ". . . that the rate of progress is such that an individual human being, of ordinary length of life, will be called upon to face novel situations which find no parallel in his past. The fixed person for the fixed duties, who in older societies was such a godsend, in the future will be a public danger."

"There will be no rolling back to an agrarian age," adds Dr. Charles R. DeCarlo, education director for I B M. "We must give people wider-based skills and education. We must give a person the analytical ability which will enable him to shift from one job to another, to take with him skills which can be applied to the new job and to pick up things which are new."

"Men will spend less time shuffling paper," says John Diebold, the automation consultant. "The information you need will be available, and there will be more emphasis on using it creatively."

"All too often," concludes John W. Gardner, "we are giving young people cut flowers when we should be teaching them to grow their own plants. We are stuffing their heads with the products of earlier innovation rather than teaching them how to innovate. We think of the mind as a storehouse to be filled rather than as an instrument to be used."

The overriding change in our job composition, brought on by computing machines, is in the explosion of human activity in research. We are entering an era of rampant curiosity, soon to unfold on a scale that, even though we know it is coming, we cannot yet adequately imagine.

Economic pessimists allow that past mechanical inventions have created new industries that dwarfed the ones they had put out of business. The automobile, which disemployed the wagonmaker and blacksmith, remade the American way of living. The invention of the cotton gin, the sewing machine, the telephone, the electric light, celluloid, the reaper, the cash register, motion pictures, the linotype, the phonograph record—each was greeted with howls of despair by those whose skills would have to shift. But the trouble is, say the economic pessimists, today there is no single growth industry based on a newfangled invention to compare with those of the good old days.

These pessimists remind one of the newspaper cub reporter who was sent to cover an American Legion meeting and came back with no story. "There was no meeting," he told his city editor. "They got into a big fist fight, and half of them were carried off to a hospital." What the pessimists fail to see is that the act of searching, discovering, inventing, is itself an industry growing so fast it is almost out of hand.

In the single year of 1963 the United States government (not counting foundations, universities, or private industry) spent more in research and development than it spent in all the time between the American Revolution and World War II—more than 12 billion dollars.

Some of the research done by private industry, like Henry Ford's tinkering with a horseless carriage, may revolutionize our lives, and some of it may be folly. But all of it reveals why an affluent society never runs out of jobs. The availability of money for doing things leads to searching for new things to do. Today the seats of a modern jetliner cost about $85,000 per pair—more than an entire airliner cost thirty years ago. Why? Because so much is spent for design research. Competition among the airlines—and their ability to pay for research—leads each to design its own seat that will be as comfortable for a 100-pound woman as for a 250-pound man, have enough buoyancy to serve as an emergency life preserver, that will not provoke allergies, and will keep looking new for its short life expectancy of a year and a half—when a new design will probably be installed.

Most government research is financed under military budgets, for that seems to be the only way to pry the money out of Congress. But many military discoveries may do more to change life in peace than in war. The Army Quartermaster Research Center recently developed a way of preserving foods by exposing it to minute amounts of radiation. The method may revolutionize the food industry by eliminating the need for refrigerating or canning of many vegetables, fruits, meats, seafood, and evaporated milk. The radiation also protects huge bins of stored wheat against insects. Aside from the obvious changes the method would work in American lives, it would make possible for the first time the shipment of bountiful quantities of good food to lands where refrigeration is absent.

Meanwhile the Navy has financed, among hundreds of other projects, a startling revolution in the production of electricity. Recently a radio transmitter was powered by bacteria feeding on sugar in a 7-inch test tube of sea water. Such "biochemical fuel cells" can draw energy from ordinary organic materials in water—including sewage that pollutes our rivers—and could eventually electrify whole cities more cheaply than hydroelectric or nuclear installations, convert nitrogen from the air and phosphorus in the sea to food and fertilizers, and end the problem of water pollution.

A ten-year-old invention called a maser (for Microwave Amplification by Simulated Emission of Radiation), which led to a four-year-old invention called a laser (for Light Amplification by Simulated Emission of Radiation), will, in the opinion of many scientists, open a proliferation of research into practical fields that had been undreamed-of by sober men for this century. A laser squeezes light waves into a microscopic, extremely powerful beam. This beam is focused energy, billions of times hotter than the surface of the sun. A laser has burned a hole through a diamond in two hundred-millionths of a second. At New York's Columbia-Presbyterian Hospital, doctors aimed another laser at a tumor on the retina of a patient's eye, and flashed it for one thousandth of a second. The tumor disappeared. As a substitute for wires and wireless radio, a laser beam, transmitted through "light pipes," will soon be able to carry a thousand TV programs or a million phone calls simultaneously, more than all the air-wave channels now in existence. The laser may even lead to making a room lamp the size of a pencil point, virtually indestructible, operating on one-tenth of the power of today's light bulb, and one that would never wear out.

The laser, still in its infancy, is already the object of

research by 400 private firms and universities, 2,000 scientists, each backed by technicians and office help, and experimental budgets of more than $30 million a year.

The growth of research as an industry is remapping America almost as the growth of great factories did a generation and two ago. "You can almost plot America's economic development in the future," James Reston of *The New York Times* pointed out recently, "by locating the Nobel prize winners in the natural sciences. There are seventeen of them in California, eleven in New York, five in Massachusetts, two in New Jersey and seven in the Middle West."

Recently Jerome B. Wiesner, former White House science adviser, scolded the Midwest for "its intellectual vacuum," demonstrated by its lack of research compared to that on each coast. The Midwest had neglected the newest of major industries, he said, because it was "comfortable and highly competent" in the old-fashioned activity of consumer production. Before long, Midwestern governors banded together to lure more research to their states. Governor Frank B. Morrison of the corn-and-cattle state of Nebraska boomed, "You can't have successful industry without having successful research."

In the spring of 1964 the National Science Foundation promised to expand the present fifteen to twenty "centers of research excellence" to double that number by 1970, making an effort to establish major new projects in areas that need the benefit of the indirect economic stimulation that research money brings.

10

the new! improved! machine-made housewife

"With all their talk about masers and lasers," a middle-aged woman enrolled at the University of Minnesota told me, "I found that when my husband brought his friends home I couldn't understand them any more. And when my son visits us from college it's the same thing. I had to go back to school just to keep from feeling the world had been pulled out from under me."

One of the immediate side effects of the technological revolution—which directly affects half the species and indirectly the other half—is the profound change it is working upon the life of the woman. A new crisis in the self-esteem and role of the housewife is apparent in the violent arguments that can be ignited at the mere mention of the name of Betty Friedan and her provocative book, *The Feminine Mystique.*

In many ways the self-examining housewife has lately been forced to face, along with the coal miner disemployed by a machine, the dreadful question of her own worthiness. Only part of her problem—perhaps a minor part—derives from the presence in her kitchen and laundry room of gleaming white machines to perform the drudgery that used to earn the Good Conduct Medal of motherhood. The major part of the problem may be subtler, and harder to solve, than that. Her husband still measures a devoted wife against the image of his Mom. But the husband hardly expects to be like his Daddy. Father was a wage worker; the son is a salaried, decision-making professional. Father quit high school to learn a trade; son went through the university. Thus his wife's dilemma. How is a woman to be an old-style 16-hour-a-day cook, laundress, house cleaner, and child-rearer—like Mom—and at the same time be an educated husband's stimulating companion? The solution chosen by many women has led to a spreading of the educational explosion into the home as well as the factory, office, and laboratory. There is a growing stampede of women back to school.

Many are headed for Sarah Lawrence College and Barnard and Radcliffe, the University of Kansas City, and, most especially, the University of Minnesota. Each of these schools has received a grant from the Carnegie Corporation to test what can be done to add fresh educational interests to the lives of married women. Each was stunned by the enthusiasm and size of the response from women who seemed to have been waiting for just this opportunity.

Sarah Lawrence announced in January 1962 through a tiny article in *The New York Times* that the following

September it would interview mature women who wanted to attend special daytime seminars. The college also offered to counsel housewives about courses in other schools in New York, Connecticut, and New Jersey. Some one hundred phone calls greeted the announcement the day it appeared; two hundred and fifty letters arrived within a week; interviews began eight months ahead of schedule.

In another experiment, Radcliffe College at Cambridge, Massachusetts, offers fellowships to a few women with Ph. D.'s or superior professional achievement, so they may pay for household help and spend part time in serious advanced study. Radcliffe also organized daytime seminars for women who seek stimulation but not college credit, and so did the University of Kansas City. Rutgers University in New Jersey has experimented, under a Ford Foundation grant, with a course to equip women college graduates for jobs in mathematics. Barnard College invited women with old college diplomas to hear lectures on what's new in professional careers and how women may tune up for them; half the applicants had to be turned away.

But nowhere has an experiment caught on as at the University of Minnesota. Twelve hundred women have flocked to that campus to sign up in the Women's Continuing Education Program, known as the Minnesota Plan. Of all the experiments, the Minnesota Plan is the least specialized, the most open to any woman qualified for college courses, no matter what her background or her aims. The entire campus is thrown open to mature married women. They enroll in the same classes as young coeds and football heroes. Yet, unlike regular students, they may take as little as one course if that's all their home schedules allow. This is almost unheard of in other daytime colleges and universities. Mothers of preschool children have even organized a Minnesota Plan cooperative nursery.

"These women who say that modern appliances have not given them more time," asks one Minnesota student, Katherine Holmberg, "what do they spend their time doing?" Mrs. Holmberg has excellent qualifications to pose the question. She earned a degree in home economics more than thirty years ago, taught the subject for two years, then married and had children. Today, in her fifties, she commutes eighty miles from Mankato, Minnesota, to the university to study for a master's degree in a combination of home economics and social work. She wants to get a job instructing women from deprived homes in techniques of good homemaking.

"For years some women resisted automatic washers," she says. "I could hardly wait to get mine. I never tried to rationalize that a good cake can only be made from scratch when the obvious fact is that cake mixes are excellent. Maybe the difference is that some of us really want time outside the kitchen to do things like study—and others don't.

"In the last fifteen years I've experienced several generations of change—from real drudgery to pushbutton living. Right after the war, during the housing shortage, we moved into a log cabin built to be a summer cottage. The only plumbing was a drain in the kitchen sink. On dark winter nights we wrote Christmas cards by oil lamp, the kids did homework by flashlight in bed. *That* was drudgery.

"Now we have additional rooms, new appliances, everything. I *know* how much time appliances save, especially when the kids are grown up and gone. I don't know how other women spend the time their appliances save, but I spent mine in reading and politics. I got so active I was elected a delegate to the state Republican convention. I became president of the P T A Council of Mankato.

"That kind of work had its satisfactions. But in community work you never know if you are doing something meaningful or just keeping busy. The work can make you feel important, but you never know if you're really qualified or competent—if you're really *worthy*."

What Mrs. Holmberg was saying had become quite familiar to Mrs. Esther Raushenbush, former dean of Sarah Lawrence College, who now directs Sarah Lawrence's Women's Continuing Education Center. "Over and over again," she says, "I keep hearing the same phrase about volunteer community work, 'Yes, I know it's important but I've *had* it.' After years of it, a certain kind of woman seeks a satisfaction that volunteer work doesn't give her. She almost always has trouble expressing it—as though it's a forbidden thing to say. When you finally pin it down, she wants to do something professional instead of something amateur. Instead of just the recognition of her neighbors, she may want professional recognition—and compensation—to show that her work has real worth."

Under the Minnesota Plan, women are reaching these goals right along. One graduate of the program, a mother of six, had earned a degree as a chemist before she was married. That was twenty years ago, and she hadn't stepped into a lab since. She returned to school for a few courses and, in less than a year, was working as a chemist in a research lab. Lucille Fackler, in her early fifties, decided to qualify for a teaching certificate. Today, she is teaching business skills to unemployed adults in the federal labor-retraining program. Mary Ann Hove and Eunice Olson are teaching in Minneapolis public schools, although only two years ago a college degree seemed a remote dream. Another graduate is running a nursery school. Mrs. Helen Niedere enrolled in a postgraduate seminar for nurses, to help equip her for rehabilitating alcoholics. A minister's wife earned a degree she had always wanted and now feels that she is a more valuable assistant to her husband.

An example is Mrs. Janet Davison, thirty-seven, a St. Paul, Minnesota, mother of three. "After ten years of drudgery on every committee in town, being chairman of this and that, frankly I got bored," she says. Before her marriage she had been a kindergarten teacher, qualified by two years of college. In 1960 Mrs. Davison had a strong desire to reenter her profession. Under new laws, she needed a bachelor's degree, but her old certificate qualified her to teach as a substitute. She decided to see if the classroom still attracted her.

"It did. One day a principal, Evelyn Pearson, stepped into a second-grade class to observe me teaching. She asked if I had a degree. When I told her no, she didn't seem to believe me. 'You're too good to be substituting,' she told me. 'You've got zing.' Well, I can tell you, *that* was enough to motivate me right back to school."

The Minnesota Plan was then just in its launching phase, so when Mrs. Davison inquired at the university, a regular student counselor examined her school record, asked no questions about her home life, the ages of her children, the attitude of her husband. These, after all, were Mrs. Davison's problems, not the university's. "You can take fifteen credits," the counselor told her, "and you can have your degree in a year and a half."

Mrs. Davison was shocked. *Fifteen credits?* That was a study load to keep a young co-ed at her books day and night.

Later that day Mrs. Davison attended a meeting of the

American Association of University Women. The speaker happened to be a psychologist, Dr. Virginia Senders, who was trying to encourage housewives to go back to college. But the picture she painted was different from the one Mrs. Davison had observed that morning. Dr. Senders described what she was then helping to get started, called the Minnesota Plan.

The new scheme, Dr. Senders explained, was mostly an attitude. It recognized the obvious but widely ignored fact that a mother going back to daytime college is no teen-age, dormitory-housed, full-time coed. She has to meet other demands too. Both school and student need to adjust their old ways to accommodate each other.

Next day Mrs. Davison was working out a schedule with Anita Smith, a Minnesota Plan counselor.

"Now remember," the counselor said, "with the demands of being a mother, keeping house, and half-time substitute teaching, you have a full-time job even without your study. Also remember you haven't been in school for ten years. It's a different pace. You have to take it slowly at first. Why don't you start with one course—at most two—and see how you do?"

As word of the Minnesota Plan spread, many wives of university professors turned up for counseling. "Why in the world," wondered co-director Vera Schletzer, "do they, of all people, need our help?" Then Mrs. Schletzer realized that a large university is so complicated it sometimes intimidates even a wife whose life revolves around it. No wonder, she thought, that rules and expectations baffled women who had not set foot on a campus in years.

In the Davison household, going to school became contagious. Janet's husband, a railroad sales agent, decided that he too would return and get a few credits he was lacking for graduation. In June 1962, at the age of thirty-eight, he earned his bachelor of arts degree.

Mrs. Davison admits to an uncertainty, however.

"I can't help feeling uneasy about what my neighbors think when they see me leaving the house in the morning —as a man does. At parties, they ask about it. You can't quite tell if they're jealous or resentful or what."

"The trouble is," explains Bonnie Nelson, a mother of three who is studying psychology, "that women are not really sure that going to school is womanly. A woman knows she's being womanly if she's thinking about her home or her community. But if she admits to strong feelings about outside subjects, she feels peculiar. She's not being feminine."

Yet, there are signs of change. Around Minneapolis, a trend acquires status when it wins acceptability in the smart, wealthy suburb of Wayzata. And lately in Wayzata the "thing to do" is to enroll in Minnesota Plan daytime seminars for women, such as "Cultivation of Vision" (on art) or "New Worlds of Knowledge" (on new developments in science and social thought). Such social pacesetters as Katharine Pillsbury (the name Pillsbury around Minneapolis is like the name Ford around Detroit), wives of company presidents, professors, and psychiatrists, have been enrolled, along with wives of salesmen and engineers. The seminars are not, heaven forbid, designed to prepare for gainful employment, but for "self-enrichment." Still, they make it easier for other women to pursue learning for practical purposes without doubting their womanliness.

The ultimate hope of Elizabeth Cless, codirector of the Minnesota Plan, is that colleges will stop viewing an education as something that is acquired completely in a

continuous effort of four years between the ages of seventeen and twenty-two, particularly since women often
interrupt schooling for marriage and never resume.

"If schools would teach young girls," says Mrs. Cless, "to
look upon college as something to return to, a woman
would see that a discontinuous pattern can be a great
advantage. She has repeated opportunities to make important choices. She forms an idea of how she's going to
spend her life when she first enters college. Then she may
revise her ideas when she gets married. After her children
are off her apron strings, she can change her mind again.
Each time is a new beginning. How lucky can you get?

For the housewife—whether she's interested in re-
turning to study or not—who glances longingly out her
kitchen window toward the strange, bustling, glamorous
world of paying jobs, the 1960s are a confusing time.

What is happening out there? Do any of those busy-
busy men who run offices, stores, public institutions, really
have use for a woman who packed away her diploma with
her first maternity dress? A woman who for ten, fifteen,
maybe twenty years has been low-rating herself as "just a
housewife"?

She reads in the newspapers that unemployment, already up in the millions, is inching higher. ("Then who
needs me?") She turns to an inside page and discovers that
there is a dangerous shortage of skilled workers. (And she
muses, "Good, then who *does* need me?")

Modern technology, masculine-sounding a term though
it may be, is welcoming more and more women to a
working world. As machines become more complicated,
they free human beings to become more human: more
educated, more devoted to physical health, more engaged
in helping others in the pursuit of happiness. These are the

traditional concerns of the homemaker and mother—as bearer of the culture and minister to the needs of others—but they are becoming, more and more, the professional concerns of society.

After the great shifts of working Americans from farm to factory early in this century, and the shift in the forties and fifties from factory to office, the mass movement of the sixties is to what are called the "service occupations." Service means more than waiting on tables and waxing other people's floors. It means the engagement of people of the most advanced training, as well as the simplest, in improving the lives of others.

In 1963 President John F. Kennedy published a 200-page report on the nation's manpower. First among the nation's growing critical shortages the report mentioned that of teachers; next, of medical workers—nurses, medical researchers, hospital aides; and of people trained in the social sciences—psychologists, social workers, counselors. These are occupations in which women have always felt at home.

But women are feeling more and more at home in many jobs. In 1890 less than one American wife in twenty held a job. By 1950, after World War II had altered our work patterns, one wife in four was working outside the home. Perhaps the Russian example affected us. We kept reading that among Russian doctors women outnumbered men, that Russia used women in almost every occupation. In any event, by 1960 one in three American wives was working for pay. The proportion of mothers who had gone to work after their youngest children entered school was even greater: two out of five. Under Secretary of Labor Esther Peterson flatly declares, "The increased participation of married women in the labor force is the most important employment trend in the country today."

What are the opportunities that the current job revolution is opening for women?

Hospitals and Public Health. In Charlotte, North Carolina, Mrs. Jewell Howell, mother of six, after enrolling her youngest child in school, decided to learn practical nursing. At her county's new community college, Mrs. Howell wrote on her application, "I need to be needed, and the children no longer require my full-time attention." A year later Mrs. Howell passed her state licensing examination with one of the highest scores on record.

Besides satisfying herself, she helped satisfy a nation-wide need for nurses. For example, in San Diego, California, despite an unemployment rate of 7 per cent, the state employment service foresees trouble in filling 1,-700 medical jobs that will open each year for the next few years. Most needed are registered and practical nurses, nurses' aides, and hospital orderlies. There are unfilled jobs for occupational therapists and assistants, laboratory technicians, operating-room aides, medical-records clerks, medical secretaries, hospital supervising housekeepers, dental assistants and technicians. Every state, every city, virtually every hospital in America reports similar shortages of trained people.

Why are these jobs going begging? Close to 90 per cent of all hospital patients today are covered by hospitalization insurance. Without insurance, many would have stayed home for lack of money, perhaps overlooking their symptoms altogether. Hospital admissions are further increased by new techniques in diagnosing and treating diseases.

To meet the need for staff people, hospital officials have been welcoming nurses, practical nurses, and aides on *part-time* schedules, making the opportunities especially attractive to many homemakers. Jobs requiring extensive training are being broken down into specialized fractions that can be taught in less time. Take, for example, the scrub nurse, who works with surgeons in the operating room, using only part of a nurse's training in patient care. Hillcrest Medical Center in Tulsa, Oklahoma, and a few others, have successfully trained unemployed women as operating-room technicians, a newly invented job classification that embraces specialized duties formerly left to nurses. The course lasts twenty-six weeks. Similar courses in other cities have prepared housewives for jobs as medical technicians and medical-records technicians.

The woman desiring advanced professional training is particularly sought after. When Winifred Morris, a Minneapolis housewife, enrolled for postgraduate courses in audiology, her name was given to a nearby school for the handicapped in hearing. The school implored her to take a job teaching deaf children, while she studied, offering to pay for her summer school to speed her teacher certification. The public-school system promised her a job when her courses were completed. To add to her feeling that she was the world's most wanted woman, Mrs. Morris learned of—and qualified for—a federal grant offered by the Office of Vocational Rehabilitation to finance her study. (Such grants are available in many fields of advanced training, as a counselor in any sizable college can explain.) For twelve months Mrs. Morris received $200 a month, which paid for her tuition, books, and the salary of a part-time housekeeper to care for the Morris's two preschool children.

Mental Health. In her first month of learning to be a psychiatric technician, Mrs. Eva Lee Knight of San Diego, a sparkling-eyed mother of one child, saved a life—or so she was told. She had been assigned to spend several days in a hospital ward being friendly with—and keeping a careful watch on—a patient considered suicidal. One morning the patient said, "Thanks for being so interested in me. In the last few days I was going to try something dangerous. But I think the feeling has passed now."

The job of psychiatric technician is an invention of doctors in charge of San Diego psychiatric hospitals. Mainly, the one-year training schedule was adapted from the course in vocational (practical) nursing, by dropping instruction in obstetrics and substituting a concentrated dosage of psychiatric principles. The doctors expect that in a year or two the state will establish a specialized license for psychiatric technician equivalent to the one for vocational nursing.

Shorter courses—sixteen weeks in length—to train psychiatric nurses' aides are being given in ten hospitals around the country, mainly for the unemployed eligible under the federal Manpower Development and Training Act. (Any state employment service office will explain eligibility for such training.) One hospital alone, at Dixon, Illinois, has hired 200 graduates from such courses.

At Marianna, Florida, seventy-five people, mostly unemployed women, have been trained for another newly "invented" occupation that has captured the interest of mental health authorities. At the Sunland Training Center for mentally retarded children these people were trained to be "cottage parents," in an attempt to enrich the children's lives as well as satisfy their physical needs. The course, carefully worked out by the Southern Regional Education Board, covers causes and effects of mental retardation, child development, techniques of physical care, ward management, social relationships, and emotional problems.

Perhaps the most remarkable job-creating experiment in the psychiatric field was one recently completed by Dr.

Margaret J. Rioch, a psychologist at the National Institutes of Health, Bethesda, Maryland. With the twin aims of bringing down the cost of psychiatric help and improving the usefulness of women with good general educations, Dr. Rioch led the training of eight mothers, all about the age of forty, in professional psychotherapy. The training took two years. All of the women are now employed as psychotherapists in recognized institutions. A second stage of this program was recently started at Washington, D. C., Children's Hospitals to train women as psychotherapists for disturbed children and their parents.

Medical Research. Between 1954 and 1960 the number of scientists engaged in medical research doubled, jumping from 20,000 to 40,000. By 1970 the number will double again. In 1950 the United States invested $148 million in medical research, public and private funds combined. By 1961, the figure had risen to $890 million; investment is expected to reach $3 billion by 1970.

"We're just opening the door," says Clifford F. Johnson, an official of the National Institutes of Health. "We're pitifully uninformed about what is normal as well as what is abnormal, on what health is as well as disease. Who has ever studied the normal development of a child from conception to maturity? We're just beginning to create the bench marks of health."

Every medical-research scientist—M. D. or Ph. D.— must be backed up by laboratory technicians. Any woman training for such work at a community college or vocational school will find her skills sought after.

Medical research gives us another example of "labor-saving" machines such as computers creating more jobs than they eliminate. The computer's ability to deal with masses of data allows scientists to pose fundamental questions that used to be unanswerable. For example, in one of the 15,000 research projects supported by the National Institutes of Health, scientists are forming detailed records of 50,000 mothers from early pregnancy through delivery, and examining their babies from birth through school age. The resulting computations, it is hoped, will develop clues to the causes of cerebral palsy, mental retardation, defects of the nervous system, congenital deafness and blindness. Before the advent of the computer, so massive a collection of tiny facts—such as complete records of the pregnant mother's diet, rate of smoking, extent of exercise—could not be undertaken.

Technicians to Scientists. Jean Lovin of Charlotte, North Carolina, wife of an unskilled worker and mother of three small children, took a roundabout way home one afternoon after her work as a loom operator in a hosiery mill. Stopping at the Charlotte Community College, she inquired about a course in bookkeeping. A school counselor, after administering aptitude tests, suggested that Mrs. Lovin learn electronic data processing with a possibility of advancing to computer programing. Employers, the counselor pointed out, are waiting in line for graduates of a one-year training course.

"After I enrolled," Mrs. Lovin reports, "my children developed a real interest in arithmetic, because they heard me talking math so much. And my husband caught my excitement. Now he's enrolled in a data-processing class too."

Despite the "labor-saving" use of computers, the designing of one jet—the Convair 880—stepped up a demand for thousands with technical skills, many of them women. A Convair official, Frank Hunter, traveled over half the United States to recruit 1,200 technical illustrators to draw pictures of the plane's individual parts for its service manual. The manual is so voluminous that its pages would make a stack twelve feet high. New jets, space ships, computers, robots, complex machines—all are designed with the help of hundreds of technical illustrators and technical writers. Their skills can be learned in a year or two, and will be useful for a lifetime in an automated era.

Today Hunter teaches technical illustration at San Diego City Junior College. About 40 per cent of his students are women. Eager employers will give many of them part-time work in their own homes. A similar course is taught in virtually every sizable city's vocational schools and community colleges.

Women who study further, earning degrees in math, the physical sciences, foreign languages, will find many doors opening for them. College graduates of years past may qualify for new jobs by taking a few refresher courses. The need for people of advanced training has all but crushed the traditional male resistance to hiring women for scientific and technical jobs.

In government, for example, Barbara Shute, a young physicist at the Goddard Space Flight Center in Maryland, selected the launch time for Explorer XII. Mrs. Melba Roy, a mathematician, supervises four women and seven men in producing advanced orbital programs. Mrs. Roy likes the sciences because work is "evaluated on its quality, and extraneous factors are eliminated." The "extraneous factor" of being a woman may not be all Mrs. Roy has in mind. As a Negro, she has always had to overcome discrimination. The group she heads was recently honored for being "incredibly accurate" in its scientific computations.

About four hundred women hold scientific and technical jobs with the National Aeronautics and Space Administration; thousands more are employed by private contractors who do 90 per cent of N A S A's scientific work. In research of all kinds, the need for scientists, mathematicians, and linguists is so great that virtually every large college offers government loans to encourage advanced study. In some cases, the loans need not be repaid if the student becomes a teacher.

Women torn between the attractions of the health sciences and space need not choose one over the other. Biologists, chemists, physiologist, psychologists, all are needed in space research. Daisy Fields, a personnel official of N A S A, says, "We have to find out how to survive on the moon if we're ever going to get there and get back."

Education. The shortage of schoolteachers is well known. By 1970, we will need half a million more than were needed in 1960. Thousands of teaching posts are now filled by "permanent substitutes," teachers who lack the necessary college credits for regular jobs; schools must hire whomever they can get. Any woman who has graduated from college, no matter when, or who went far toward graduation, is at most only a few course credits away from earning certification as a schoolteacher. Thousands of mothers have launched careers as teachers after enrolling their last child in school.

Some pioneering schools have sought to ease the shortage by relieving teachers of specialized tasks, in the same way that hospitals substitute technicians for nurses. Las Vegas, Nevada, recently trained forty mothers, some with only high-school diplomas, to be teacher's aides. Beverly Mackie, a mother of four, has graded papers for a health class, run a duplicating machine to produce study materials, and used her experience as a ceramics hobbyist in helping to teach art. Romaine Scott, mother of two, runs a high-school audiovisual room, replacing a teacher in making slides, splicing films and tapes, maintaining supplies and typing. These women get home about the same time their own school children do, and have the same holidays off, so family life has hardly changed.

In related fields, the need for librarians is so great that many libraries are employing aides trained on the job for specialized tasks. At the Austin, Texas, public library, mothers working part time make up more than half of the library staff.

The "cultural explosion" accompanying America's education expansion is opening new fields of paid work to enrich the use of leisure time. Administrators of art museums, symphony orchestras, cultural centers, are in short supply. Universities have trouble finding organizers of adult education. Editorial writers are in great demand. Travel agencies are always searching for qualified staff. Recently, housing developments have begun to offer organized recreation under a paid director to attract buyers. As the resort industry expands, direction of recreation will expand as a profession.

Child Care. Of all the expanding occupations for women, there is one that few mothers realize can be made a career: the care of children. California is a pioneer in providing state support for 234 child-care centers for 25,-000 children of working mothers in low-income families. Some are preschoolers, others go to child-care centers before and after school hours. Normally, parents pay one-third of the cost of child care, the rest being paid from public funds. Theresa Mahler, director of twenty-five San Francisco centers, points out that the centers are run by licensed nursery and school teachers. Good day care, she emphasizes, must be an educational experience, not mere baby sitting, especially for the preschooler from an economically and culturally deprived home. In other cities, standards for the training requirements of a child-care staff are less strict.

The California plan is expected to spread to other areas, but interest is stretching beyond the care of children in low-income families. For example, with increasing frequency Mrs. Mahler receives calls from mothers in high-income Marin County across the Golden Gate Bridge. Educated women eager to use their training in professional jobs ask, "What can we do to start child-care centers of our own?" Thus the growing interest of women in finding jobs for pay may soon create a multitude of paying jobs in child care.

Homemaking for Pay. Some 3 million American women are engaged as housekeeping workers. Surveys by manpower experts show that more jobs would be available if the tens of thousands of unemployed women looking for housework were trained to be really good at it. Recently the federal government began encouraging communities to start classes in professional housekeeping. In San Francisco, after a survey showed there were job openings for trained housekeepers, a class was launched offering unemployed women 850 hours of detailed instruction in cleaning, cooking, child care, and personal habits.

Other government manpower studies show growing employment opportunities for trained women as food-service workers, homemaker-companions for the elderly, and visiting homemakers for mothers who are ill or on vacation.

The lack of homemaking skills among many unemployed women is itself giving rise to an important new occupation. The New York Department of Welfare employs 326 homemaking instructors to teach impoverished mothers the rudiments of bringing order to seemingly hopeless households: how to clean, cook, sew, make beds, change diapers, do the laundry, plan shopping, and spend wisely. Many cities are discovering the widespread need for such teaching and are beginning to provide it for families on welfare rolls.

The New Volunteer. Even women's volunteer work is becoming more professional. Many women's organizations are tiring of their "make-work" ways of the past, and are seeking real needs of the community to fill with intelligent, skilled services.

In St. Louis, suburban members of the Council of Jewish Women volunteered to train as nursery workers and serve the city's board of education in a nationally significant experiment. They conducted nursery classes for four- and five-year-old Negro slum children as early preparation for successful schooling.

In Norfolk, Virginia, women volunteers are working with the city health department in a 20-block Negro slum area to staff a well-baby and immunization clinic as part of a massive attack on poverty. In almost every large city, at least one resourceful women's group has located a challenging problem of society and is devoting itself in a professional way to improving the lives of the needy.

Many of today's new professions for women were the volunteer activities of yesterday. Today's important volunteer work may become the professional work of tomorrow as its importance is proved by the volunteers.

11

the urban agrarians

Almost imperceptibly during the past couple of years an important public awareness has taken hold. When talk turns to automation and the unemployed, someone says with a sigh of worriment, "Yes, we've got to do something about teaching those people skills."

It ought to be said in tones of triumph instead of worriment. But the fact that the comment is made at all is remarkable. What it implies—even though its implications have not yet dawned on many—is that there's hardly anything wrong with our economy that a bit of education won't cure. Witness the staggering change from the thirties, when unemployment last preoccupied us. No present talk of overproduction, underconsumption, vicious economic cycles, closed factory gates, clubbing of labor pickets, recruiting of the desperately unemployed as strikebreakers, brutal exploitation of man by man. Can anyone imagine walking the length of a breadline in 1933, taking count of the gaunt faces and wasted talent, and saying, "Their trouble is that they didn't finish high school"? Hardly any observation in that time of economic paralysis, when there seemed to be almost nothing for anyone to do, could have been more irrelevant.

But a new danger today is the lulling, comforting idea that all we have to do to spread the wealth is a little teaching of skills among those who somehow missed out on them. That simple prescription brings solace to everyone except those who need it most, the men and women hopelessly out of jobs.

We have seen in the episode of Don Jones—as repeated in the lives of tens of thousands—how much good a "little teaching of skills" can do—if the student is prepared for training. We have seen in the case of the Chicago welfare recipients—an action story that several cities are now trying to emulate—how much good some teaching of the basic language can do in preparing people for learning a skill. But we have seen, too, that tens of thousands of adults, prepared in these limited ways for entering the world of self-reliance, are annually supplanted in the world of dependence by hundreds of thousands of children from degraded schools in city and country who have no prospect of fitting themselves for today's needs.

Economists have been debating whether unemployment of so many young people is "cyclical"—due to ups and downs of business conditions—or "structural"—because the abilities of the unemployed are out of gear with current job openings. But the evidence suggests that today's chronic unemployment is not adequately described by either the word "cyclical" or the word "structural." A better term would be "cultural unemployment."

To get at the root of the widespread human uselessness that we mistakenly ascribe to automation, we must look into a vast *cultural* chasm that separates the successfully employed from the so-called unemployable. They are living in different centuries—the culture of each separated from the other's by a hundred and fifty years of history. In today's American city we find some who have successfully emerged from the factory system into the age of technology, science, research, abstract symbols, and art—and others who have not yet entered the stage of economic history we call the factory system, which got under way in the early nineteenth century. Although city dwellers, these "unemployables" have the characteristics of the preurban, prefactory villager of the agrarian age.

Let's list some cultural traits of the "undesirables" in the modern city that provide fuel for anti-Negro prejudice, disdain for the white mountaineer, contempt for most of the chronically poor: unwillingness to forsake familiar poverty in search of something better; lack of sustained work discipline; a surface appearance of childlike happy-go-luckiness, accompanied by an unawareness of the "importance" of time; a penchant for unpredictably quitting a job and taking one's sweet time before looking for another; lack of ambition, as we define the word in middle-class American culture.

These phrases, in the modern American context, suggest the stereotypes of poor Negroes, Puerto Ricans, "hillbillies"—the "culturally deprived." But I have drawn the list not from American sterotypes. It is taken from an account of life among English villagers in the 1810s to 1830s. In those decades, owners of the earliest factories were trying, with great frustration, to lure rural folk into factory work.

As this frustration is vividly summed up by Sebastian de Grazia in his exhaustive study for the Twentieth Century Fund, *Of Time, Work, and Leisure,* one could easily be misled into thinking he was reading about today's American "unemployables." De Grazia says "It was like pulling a molar barehanded to get the villager out of his home. . . . If he moved to find work, it was often to the nearest village. . . . If he went too far out and stayed away he might lose the chance of the poorhouse. Even when a model employer or factory appeared on the scene to offer help to villagers near starvation, as rarely occurred, they chose their customary state. They might go with all their children to the factory with higher wages and steadier employment and get installed in the comfortable quarters provided them, but after a few weeks the going was too much.

"Though they might be weavers and the factory a spinning mill, the new work habits required of them went against the grain. They returned to their bit of land, rented or owned, which they worked long in summer, short in winter. . . . Here there was no having to stay with the unfeeling machine until someone shut off the power. The life they knew was unpunctual and chatty. A shoemaker got up in the morning when he liked and began work when he liked. If anything of interest happened, out he went from his stool to take a look himself. If he spent too much time at the alehouse drinking and gossiping one day, he made up for it by working till midnight the next. Like the Lapons or the Trobriand Islanders he worked by enthusiastic spurts and spent long periods without toil, which among nonindustrial communities is a way of working more common than is generally supposed. . . .

As factory workers these early employees left much for the employer to desire. The rural mentality was always with them."

It is natural that today's urban indigent has the outlook of an agrarian. For the chances are that that is what he is. He either came from a small, impoverished family farm or has lived his life segregated among—and absorbing the culture of—parents, relatives, and neighbors who did.

Transplanted to city slums, the culture of the country poor, admirable as it may be in its natural setting, can no longer usefully serve its human bearers. But, insulated by ghetto walls, neither can it absorb and blend with urban culture, to which slum dwellers are almost never permitted real access.

How can we hope, under the time pressure of present-day unemployment, to change overnight the ingrained ways of men and women in their forties, fifties, sixties? The hard truth must be faced that we can't. We must try to save them from misery in their remaining years by such stopgaps as job training for lower skills, literacy training, devices such as a tax cut that may boost the demand for the kinds of low drudgery that one day few human beings will be asked to perform.

Ghettos of the ignorant poor are like a basement flooded by a burst waterpipe. Something must be done, of course, about the knee-deep water. But even more urgent than this short-range problem is the need to put an end to the long-range threat of disaster: the first thing one must do in a flooded basement is turn a valve to shut off the running water.

No matter how urgently our sense of humanity moves us to alleviate today's unemployment, we must not be distracted from the greater urgency of trying to prevent tomorrow's and the day after tomorrow's.

The method, overwhelming a challenge as it presents, is described simply: we must no longer permit any American child born after the middle of the twentieth century to be subjected to an early nineteenth-century education. We must stop the production of prefactory agrarians for a postfactory, scientific, intellectual society.

What does this mean?

1. It means that when a school in Mississippi continues to schedule its school year and pitch its curriculum on the assumption that its pupils will follow careers in cotton-picking, and when a school system continues to price a young American's education at less than $200 a year, as many Southern schools do, the matter is no longer one of mere local concern but of national crisis.

2. It means that when a lady school superintendent in a rural, ex-coal-mining county of Kentucky protects her children's "purity of heart" by opposing factory jobs in her county, the matter is a concern of Cincinnati, Chicago, Detroit, and New York. The local welfare funds of metropolitan cities will soon support these children as jobless school dropouts, and, later, their offspring, all probable inheritors of poverty.

3. It means that schools of the city slums must come to the realization that not bigger budgets nor smaller classes nor sleeker buildings will by themselves correct the failure to interest young minds that are trapped in the segregated culture of the new urban agrarians. Their education must begin by reeducating their teachers. If any crash program to help educate today's slum children will work, perhaps it will be a crash program to help teachers understand the special needs of their students as urban-agrarians. No program for such mass training of thousands of teachers appears at present on the horizon, even though it would be far more practical an undertaking

than the seemingly hopeless task of trying to cram book-learning into millions of unwilling young minds.

4. It means that many Americans must reexamine their feelings about the civil-rights movement. They must recognize that Negro demands are the only avenue for Negroes to escape from perpetual economic dependence on the welfare taxes of their white fellow citizens. The Negro revolution is not a political event that just happened to happen now. It comes at a time when mechanization of the cotton field and factory makes it impossible for uneducated Negroes to continue to live by subhuman toil. If they are not to die as dependent as slaves, they must fight for the right to more desirable work. This means they must fight for their right to be schooled and their right of access to the middle-class niceties associated with more desirable work. The civil-rights movement is one of the clear-cut evidences of how machines not only *permit* the wider flourishing of higher human values, but indeed *require* them to flourish more widely.

If human knowledge is fast becoming the most important capital resource of our economy, we have to take a new look at ways to develop our national wealth. The sound old business advice of "plowing profits back into developing the business" should now be updated to "plowing profits back into developing people." The development of people is the new national business of America.

Men who make public policy, liberals and conservatives alike, therefore, must revise some of their old habits of mind. These habits were born in the thirties and earlier, when factory and farm drudgery were the main engagement of the people.

We have learned by now for example, that public spending for welfare and make-work projects, traditionally supported by liberals, even though it may alleviate the immediate pains of poverty, often perpetuates poverty. Welfare and make-work do nothing to equip the poor for reentering a society of ascending skills as self-supporting, self-respecting citizens. If liberals are ready to adjust to the new realities of a machine-shaped society, they would do well to start regarding with a skeptical eye—as conservatives traditionally have done—any aid to the able-bodied poor that prolongs dependence.

Liberals can consider such a change of stance, however, only if conservatives revise their traditional policy of opposing government spending on the poor, almost without regard to how the money is to be spent. Spending for improved education and job training—including the support of families while a breadwinner is being trained— cannot be regarded as a down-the-drain expense but must be seen as a national investment. It develops the profitability of our chief economic resource—human talent —and, in fact, rapidly pays off by converting welfare recipients and rocking-chair-money collectors into cash-money taxpayers.

Increased public investment in the universal education of human beings—with guarantees of full equality of opportunity which do not now exist—is consistent with the past aims of conservatives as well as liberals, Democrats as well as Republicans. All lawmakers, in considering the requirements of a new, machine-shaped society, should ask of any new welfare proposal, "Will it improve the ability of human beings?"

When the compassion of the liberal and the prudent practicality of the conservative unite in a quest that befits them both—a search for ways to invest in the improvement of the abilities of our own people—we will have begun to fulfill the highest purpose not only of the machine, but of man, who invented it and was elevated by it.

bibliography for suggested additional reading

Berkeley, Edmund C., *The Computer Revolution.* (Garden City, New York; Doubleday, 1962)

Brown, B. Frank, *The Nongraded High School.* (Englewood Cliffs, N. J.; Prentice-Hall, 1963)

Buckingham, Walter, *Automation: Its Impact on Business and People.* (New York; Harper & Row, 1961)

Caudill, Harry M., *Night Comes to the Cumberlands: A Biography of a Depressed Area.* (Boston; Little, Brown & Co., 1963)

Curtis, Thomas B. *87 Million Jobs.* (New York; Duell, Sloan & Pearce, 1962)

DeGrazia, Sebastian; *Of Time, Work and Leisure.* (New York; The Twentieth Century Fund, 1962)

Diebold, John, *Automation: The Advent of the Automatic Factory.* (Princeton, N. J.; D. Van Nostrand, 1952)

Dunlop, John T., *Automation and Technological Change.* (Englewood Cliffs, N. J.; Prentice-Hall, 1962)

Harrington, Michael, *The Other America.* (New York; Macmillan, 1962)

Higbee, Edward, *Farms and Farmers in an Urban Age.* (New York; The Twentieth Century Fund, 1963)

Jacobs, Paul, *Dead Horse and the Featherbird.* (New York; The Fund for the Republic, 1962)

Jacobson, Howard Boone and Roucek, Joseph S. (eds.), *Automation and Society.* (New York; Philosophical Library, 1959)

Lyford, Joseph P., *The Talk in Vandalia.* (New York, The Fund for the Republic, 1962)

Michael, Donald N., *Cybernation: The Silent Conquest.* (New York; The Fund for the Republic, 1962)

Riessman, Frank, *The Culturally Deprived Child.* (New York; Harper & Row, 1962)

Sexton, Patricia Cayo, *Education and Income.* (New York; Viking Press, 1961)

Snow, C. P., *The Two Cultures and the Scientific Revolution.* (New York; Cambridge University Press, 1959)

Wiener, Norbert, *The Human Uses of Human Beings.* (Boston, Houghton-Mifflin Co., 1950)

The Challenge of Automation. Papers delivered at the National Conference on Automation. (Washington, D.C.; Public Affairs Press, 1955)

Economic and Social Implications of Automation: A Bibliographic Review. Vols. I and II. (East Lansing, Michigan; Labor and Industrial Relations Center, Michigan State University, 1958 and 1961)

Education for a Changing World of Work. (Washington, D. C.; U. S. Department of Health, Education and Welfare; Office of Education, 1962)

Manpower Report of the President, (Washington, D. C.; U. S. Department of Labor, 1963)

New Views on Automation. (Washington, D. C.; Joint Economic Committee, Congress of the U. S., 1960)

No Room at the Bottom. (Washington, D. C.; National Education Association, 1963)

index

about the author

Since publication of his best-selling *When F.D.R. Died,* Bernard Asbell has spent more than three years and traveled over 100,000 miles studying education in the new era of computers and robots. He has served as a consultant on education to the Ford Foundation (Educational Facilities Laboratories) and the University of Illinois. He has been president of the Society of Magazine Writers and taught nonfiction writing at the University of Chicago, University of Bridgeport and the Bread Loaf Writers' Conference of Middlebury College. Mr. Asbell's reports on the changing ways of American life have been seen in *American Heritage, Harper's, Horizon, Ladies' Home Journal, McCall's Magazine, Redbook Magazine, The Reporter, The Saturday Evening Post,* and other periodicals. He lives in Wilton, Connecticut with his wife and four children.